Houghton
Mifflin
Harcourt

MATH
Expressions
Common Core

Dr. Karen C. Fuson

GRADE

5

Volume 2

This material is based upon work supported by the
National Science Foundation
under Grant Numbers
ESI-9816320, REC-9806020, and RED-935373.

Any opinions, findings, and conclusions, or recommendations expressed in this material
are those of the author and do not necessarily reflect the views of the National Science Foundation.

VOLUME 2 CONTENTS

UNIT 5 Division with Whole Numbers and Decimals

UNIT 6 Operations and Word Problems

UNIT 7 Algebra, Patterns, and Coordinate Graphs

UNIT 8 Measurement and Geometry

VOLUME 2 CONTENTS *(continued)*

© Houghton Mifflin Harcourt Publishing Company

Family Letter

Dear Family,

The main goal of Unit 5 of *Math Expressions* is to enhance skills in dividing with whole numbers and decimal numbers. Some additional goals are:

▶ to solve real world application problems,

▶ to use patterns as an aid in calculating,

▶ to use estimation to check the reasonableness of answers, and

▶ to interpret remainders.

Your child will learn and practice methods such as Place Value Sections, Expanded Notation, and Digit-by-Digit to gain speed and accuracy in multidigit and decimal division. Money examples will be used to help students understand division with decimals.

Throughout Unit 5, your child will solve real world application problems that require multidigit division. Your child will learn to estimate using rounding and other methods, and then to use estimation to determine whether answers are reasonable. Remainders will be interpreted in real world contexts, and expressed as fractions or decimals when appropriate. Students will learn to distinguish between multiplication and division in real world situations involving decimals.

If you have any questions, please call or write to me.

Sincerely,
Your child's teacher

COMMON CORE This unit includes the Common Core Standards for Mathematical Content for Number and Operations in Base Ten, 5.NBT.2, 5.NBT.3b, 5.NBT.5, 5.NBT.6, 5.NBT.7, and all Mathematical Practices.

Estimada familia:

El objetivo principal de la Unidad 5 de *Math Expressions* es reforzar las destrezas de división con números enteros y decimales. Algunos objetivos adicionales son:

▶ resolver problemas con aplicaciones a la vida diaria,

▶ usar patrones como ayuda para hacer cálculos,

▶ usar la estimación para comprobar si las respuestas son razonables, y por último,

▶ interpretar residuos.

Su niño aprenderá y practicará métodos como el de Secciones de valor posicional, Notación extendida y Dígito por dígito, para realizar divisiones de números de varios dígitos y decimales con mayor rapidez y exactitud. Como ayuda para comprender las divisiones con decimales, se usarán ejemplos de dinero.

En la Unidad 5 su niño resolverá problemas con aplicaciones a la vida diaria que requieran el uso de la división de números de varios dígitos. Aprenderá a estimar usando el redondeo y otros métodos, y luego usará la estimación para determinar si las respuestas son razonables. Los residuos se interpretarán dentro de contextos de la vida diaria y se expresarán como fracciones o decimales cuando sea apropiado. Los estudiantes aprenderán a distinguir entre la multiplicación y la división en situaciones de la vida cotidiana que involucren decimales.

Si tiene alguna duda o algún comentario, por favor comuníquese conmigo.

Atentamente,
El maestro de su niño

COMMON CORE Esta unidad incluye los Common Core Standards for Mathematical Content for Number and Operations in Base Ten, 5.NBT.2, 5.NBT.3b, 5.NBT.5, 5.NBT.6, 5.NBT.7, and all Mathematical Practices.

► Compare Division Methods

An airplane travels the same distance every day.
It travels 3,822 miles in a week. How far does the
airplane travel each day?

Rectangle Model

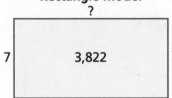

Place Value Sections

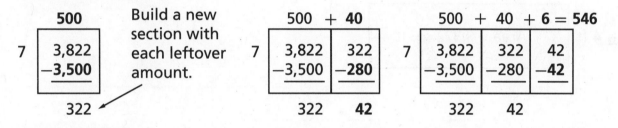

Build a new section with each leftover amount.

Expanded Notation

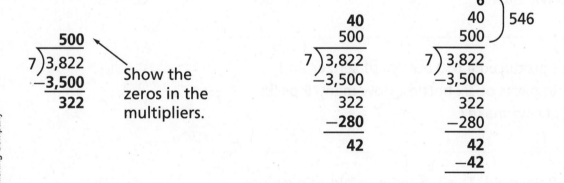

Show the zeros in the multipliers.

Digit-by-Digit

$$7\overline{)3,822}$$
$$\underline{-3,5}$$
$$32$$
quotient: 5

Put in only one digit at a time.

$$7\overline{)3,822}$$
$$\underline{-35}$$
$$32$$
$$\underline{-28}$$
$$42$$
quotient: 54

$$7\overline{)3,822}$$
$$\underline{-3,5}$$
$$32$$
$$\underline{-28}$$
$$42$$
$$\underline{-42}$$
quotient: 546

▶ Division Problems

Write an equation. Then solve.

Show your work.

1. A farmer has 2,106 cows and 9 barns. If the farmer divides the cows into equal groups, how many cows will he put in each barn?

2. A sidewalk covers 3,372 square feet. If the sidewalk is 4 feet wide, what is its length?

```
              ?
        ┌─────────────────────┐
  4 ft  │   Area = 3,372 sq. ft │
        └─────────────────────┘
```

3. Olivia has $8. Her mother has $4,784. The amount Olivia's mother has is how many times the amount Olivia has?

4. A machine produced 4,650 bottles of seltzer and put them in packs of six bottles. How many 6-packs did the machine make?

5. Raj is 3,288 days old. This is 6 times as old as his niece. How many days old is Raj's niece?

6. If a streamer is unrolled, its area is 3,888 square inches. If the streamer is 2 inches wide, how long is it?

► Work with Remainders

The problem at the right might seem unfinished. The leftover number at the bottom is called the remainder. We can write the answer like this: 567 R2.

$$
\begin{array}{r}
567 \leftarrow \text{quotient} \\
8\overline{)4{,}538} \\
-40 \\
\hline
53 \\
-48 \\
\hline
58 \\
-56 \\
\hline
2
\end{array}
$$

divisor ⟶ 8)4,538 ⟵ dividend

remainder ⟶ 2

7. Could there be a remainder of 9 for the problem? Why or why not?

_____

_____

_____

8. What is the greatest possible remainder when dividing by 8?

_____

Complete each division and give the remainder.

9. $6\overline{)5{,}380}$

10. $7\overline{)6{,}747}$

11. $5\overline{)4{,}914}$

12. $5\overline{)2{,}428}$

13. $3\overline{)2{,}972}$

14. $7\overline{)4800}$

15. $9\overline{)5{,}469}$

16. $4\overline{)3{,}183}$

17. $6\overline{)5{,}420}$

18. $8\overline{)6{,}002}$

19. $2\overline{)3{,}303}$

20. $7\overline{)4{,}000}$

▶ Use Mental Math to Check for Reasonableness

Miguel has 6 boxes to store 1,350 baseball cards.
He divides and finds that each box will have 225 cards.
To check that his answer is reasonable, he uses
estimation and mental math:

$$\begin{array}{r} 225 \\ 6\overline{)1{,}350} \end{array}$$

"I know that 1,200 ÷ 6 is 200 and 1,800 ÷ 6 is 300.
Because 1,350 is between 1,200 and 1,800, my answer
should be between 200 and 300. It is."

Solve. Then use mental math to check the solution.

21. $9\overline{)3{,}150}$

22. $3\overline{)2{,}733}$

23. $6\overline{)4{,}560}$

24. $8\overline{)7{,}136}$

25. Kim makes necklaces with colored beads. She used 1,620
   beads for 9 necklaces. How many beads did she use
   for each necklace if they have the same number of beads?

   _____

26. Saul delivers equally 1,155 newspapers in a 7-day week.
   How many newspapers does he deliver in a day?

   _____

27. Val earns $1,096 a month as a cashier. She makes $8 an hour.
   How many hours does she work in a month?

   _____

28. The Martinson School bought 1,890 water bottles to distribute
   equally among students over a 5-day period. How many bottles
   are distributed each day?

   _____

Divide Whole Numbers by One Digit

Name _____   Date _____

▶ Experiment with Two-Digit Divisors

Suppose 2,048 sheep are to be sent on a train.
Each railroad car holds 32 sheep.

To find how many railroad cars are needed for the
sheep, divide 2,048 by 32.

Rectangle Model
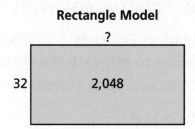

Discuss how these division methods are alike and different.

| Step 1 | Step 2 | Step 3 | Step 4 |

Digit-by-Digit

Step 1:
$$32\overline{)2,048}$$
(30)

Round the divisor.

Step 2:
$$\begin{array}{r} 6 \\ 32\overline{)2,048} \end{array}$$
(30)

Estimate the first digit:

30 goes into 200
about 6 times.

Step 3:
$$\begin{array}{r} 6 \\ 32\overline{)2,048} \\ -1\,92 \\ \hline 128 \end{array}$$
(30)

Multiply and subtract.
Bring down 8 ones.

Step 4:
$$\begin{array}{r} 64 \\ 32\overline{)2,048} \\ -1\,92 \\ \hline 128 \\ -128 \end{array}$$
(30)

Estimate the next
digit and multiply.

Expanded Notation

Step 1:
$$32\overline{)2,048}$$
(30)

Round the divisor.

Step 2:
$$\begin{array}{r} 60 \\ 32\overline{)2,048} \end{array}$$
(30)

Estimate the first number:

30 goes into 2,000
about 60 times.

Step 3:
$$\begin{array}{r} 60 \\ 32\overline{)2,048} \\ -1,920 \\ \hline 128 \end{array}$$
(30)

Multiply and subtract.
$60 \cdot 32 = 1,920$

Step 4:
$$\begin{array}{r} 4\,\}\,64 \\ 60 \\ 32\overline{)2,048} \\ -1,920 \\ \hline 128 \\ -128 \end{array}$$
(30)

Estimate the next
number and multiply.

Place Value Sections

Step 1:

60

32 | 2,048
(30)

Round the divisor
and estimate the first
number.

Step 2:

60

32 | 2,048
(30) | −1,920
_____
128

Multiply and
subtract.

Step 3:

60 +

32 | 2,048 | 128
(30) | 1,920
_____
128

Make a new
section.

Step 4:

60 + 4

32 | 2,048 | 128
(30) | −1,920 | −128
_____
128   0

Estimate the next
number, and multiply
and subtract.

▶ Experiment with Two-Digit Divisors (continued)

Look at Exercises 1–3. Would you round the divisor up or
down to estimate the first digit of the quotient?
Complete each exercise, using any method you choose.

1. 79)‾4,032‾   2. 21)‾1,533‾   3. 18)‾1,061‾

▶ Does Estimation Always Work?

Complete Exercise 4 as a class. Does rounding give you a
correct estimate of the first digit? Does it give you a correct
estimate of the next digit? Discuss what you can do to finish
the problem.

4. 54)‾3,509‾

Complete and discuss each exercise below. Use any method
you choose.

5. 74)‾3,651‾   6. 42)‾3,231‾   7. 23)‾1,892‾

VOCABULARY
overestimate
underestimate

▶ Underestimating

Here are two ways to divide 5,185 ÷ 85. Discuss each method and answer the questions as a class.

$$
\begin{array}{r}
(90)\quad 5 \\
85\overline{)5,185} \\
4\ 25 \\
\hline
93
\end{array}
$$

← What does this number tell us?

How do we know that the first estimated number is not right? What number should we try next? Solve the problem using that number.

$$
\begin{array}{r}
10 \\
(90)\quad 50 \\
85\overline{)5,185} \\
4,250 \\
\hline
935
\end{array}
$$

← What does this number tell us?

How do we know that the first estimated number is not right this time? Do we need to erase, or can we just finish solving the problem? Try it.

1. When we estimate with a number that is too big (**overestimate**), we have to erase and change the number. When we estimate with a number that is too small (**underestimate**), do we always have to erase? Explain your answer.

_____

_____

_____

Solve each division. You may need to adjust one or both of the estimated numbers.

2. $56\overline{)4,032}$ 3. $77\overline{)4,791}$ 4. $18\overline{)798}$

► Too High or Too Low?

Think about what kind of divisor is most likely to lead to an estimated number that is wrong. Test your idea by doing the first step of each problem below.

5. $41\overline{)2{,}583}$ 6. $34\overline{)1{,}525}$ 7. $29\overline{)928}$ 8. $16\overline{)1{,}461}$

9. What kind of divisor is most likely to lead to an estimated number that is wrong? How can you adjust for these cases?

_____

_____

_____

► Mixed Practice with Adjusted Estimates

Solve.   *Show your work.*

10. Hector is packing 1,375 oranges in crates that hold 24 oranges each.

    How many crates will Hector fill? _____

    How many oranges will be left over? _____

11. Skateboards sell for $76 each. This week the store sold $5,396 worth of skateboards.

    How many skateboards were sold?

    _____

12. Ashley's dog Tuffy eats 21 ounces of food for each meal. Ashley has 1,620 ounces of dog food.

    How many meals will Tuffy have before Ashley needs to buy more food? _____

    How many ounces of food will be left after the last meal? _____

▶ Decide What to Do with the Remainder

Think about each of these ways to use a remainder.

Sometimes you ignore the remainder.

1. A roll of ribbon is 1,780 inches long. It takes 1 yard of ribbon (36 inches) to wrap a gift.

   How many gifts can be wrapped?

   _____

   Why do you ignore the remainder?

   _____

   _____

Sometimes you round up to the next whole number.

2. There are 247 people traveling to the basketball tournament by bus. Each bus holds 52 people.

   How many buses will be needed?

   _____

   Why do you round up?

   _____

   _____

Sometimes you use the remainder to form a fraction.

3. The 28 students in Mrs. Colby's class will share 98 slices of pizza equally.

   How many slices will each student get?

   _____

   Look at the division shown here. Explain how to get the fraction after you find the remainder.

   _____

$$28 \overline{\smash{)}98} \quad \begin{array}{r} 3\frac{1}{2} \\ \hline -84 \\ \hline 14 \end{array}$$

▶ Decide What to Do with the Remainder (continued)

Sometimes you use a decimal number instead of the remainder.

Suppose 16 friends earned $348 at a car wash. They want to divide the money equally. The division at the right shows that each friend gets $21, and there are $12 leftover. Dividing the $12, each friend gets an additional $\frac{12}{16}$, or $\frac{3}{4}$, of a dollar, for a total of $21.75.

$$
\begin{array}{r}
21.75 \\
16\overline{)348} \\
-32 \\
\hline
28 \\
16 \\
\hline
12
\end{array}
$$

4. A rectangular garden has an area of 882 square meters. The long side of the garden has a length of 35 meters. How long is the short side?

_____

Sometimes the remainder is the answer to the problem.

5. A bagel shop has 138 bagels to be packed into boxes of 12 to be sold. The extra bagels are for the workers.

   How many bagels will the workers get?

   _____

   Why is the remainder the answer?

   _____

   _____

   _____

▶ Solve Problems Involving Remainders

Solve.

Show your work.

6. At the Cactus Flower Cafe, all the tips are divided equally among the waiters. Last night, the 16 waiters took in $1,108 in tips. How much did each waiter get?

   _____

7. A gardener needs to move 2,150 pounds of dirt. He can carry 98 pounds in his wheelbarrow. How many trips will he need to make with the wheelbarrow?

   _____

▶ Solve Problems Involving Remainders (continued)

Solve.   *Show your work.*

8. Mia must work 133 hours during the month of May. There are 21 working days in May this year. How many hours per day will Mia work if she works the same number of hours each day?

   _____

9. Colored markers cost 78 cents each. Pablo has $21.63 in his pocket. How many markers can Pablo buy?

   _____

10. A meat packer has 180 kilograms of ground meat. He will divide it equally into 50 packages. How much will each package weigh?

    _____

11. In volleyball, there are 12 players on the court. If 75 people all want to play volleyball at a gym that has more than enough courts, how many of them must sit out at one time?

    _____

12. At the Fourth of July celebration, 1,408 ounces of lemonade will be shared equally by 88 people. How many ounces of lemonade will each person get?

    _____

13. Armando needs quarters to ride the bus each day. He took $14.87 to the bank and asked to have it changed into quarters. How many quarters did he get?

    _____

Name _____ **Date** _____

▶ What's the Error?

Dear Math Students,

I am moving, and I need to pack my sardines. I have 1,700 cans of sardines, and I know I can fit 48 cans in each box.

I divided to figure out how many boxes I needed. I bought 35 boxes, but I had some cans leftover. What did I do wrong?

Your friend,
Puzzled Penguin

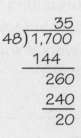

$$
\begin{array}{r}
35 \\
48\overline{)1{,}700} \\
144 \\
\hline
260 \\
240 \\
\hline
20
\end{array}
$$

14. Write a response to Puzzled Penguin.

_____

_____

_____

_____

▶ Write Your Own Problem

15. Write a word problem that involves a division that has a remainder. Solve your problem and explain what you did with the remainder in your solution.

_____

_____

_____

_____

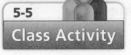
▶ Practice Dividing

Divide.

1. 6)546

2. 43)1,634

3. 5)423

4. 73)3,942

5. 5)7,016

6. 55)2,200

7. 13)9,430

8. 29)1,499

9. 3)4,040

10. 8)2,007

11. 88)6,160

12. 76)3,441

13. 41)3,605

14. 19)6,000

15. 28)8,413

▶ Solve Division Word Problems

Solve.   *Show your work.*

16. The Thomas's rectangular backyard has an area of 2,352 square feet. If the yard is 56 feet long, how wide is it?

_____

17. Milo wants to make guacamole for a party. Avocados are on sale for 84¢ each. How many avocados can Milo buy if he has $7.75?

_____

18. One quart is equal to 32 ounces. How many quarts are equal to 6,672 ounces?

_____

19. Students in the marching band sold calendars to raise money for new uniforms. Violet sold 24 calendars for a total of $186. How much did each calendar cost?

_____

20. Only 37 fans came to watch the volleyball team's first match. At the last match, 2,035 fans came to watch. The number of fans at the last match was how many times the number at the first?

_____

21. Ayala has 655 computer files she wants to put on CDs. If she can fit 18 files on each CD, how many CDs will she need?

_____

22. Ms. Adams wrote a 36-page short story that she wants to send to publishers. She buys a 500-sheet package of paper and prints as many copies of the story as she can. How many sheets does she have left over?

_____

► Divide a Decimal by a One-Digit Number

Three friends set up a lemonade stand and made $20.25.
They will share the money equally. Study the steps below to see
how much money each person should get.

When the $20 is split 3 ways, each person gets $6. There is $2 left.	We change the $2 to 20 dimes and add the other 2 dimes. There are 22 dimes.	When we split 22 dimes 3 ways, each person gets 7 dimes. There is 1 dime left.	We change the dime to 10 cents and add the other 5 cents. Now we split 15 cents 3 ways.

$$
\begin{array}{r}
6 \\
3\overline{)20.25} \\
-18 \\
\hline
2
\end{array}
\qquad
\begin{array}{r}
6. \\
3\overline{)20.25} \\
-18 \\
\hline
2.2
\end{array}
\qquad
\begin{array}{r}
6.7 \\
3\overline{)20.25} \\
-18 \\
\hline
2.2 \\
-2.1 \\
\hline
.1
\end{array}
\qquad
\begin{array}{r}
6.75 \\
3\overline{)20.25} \\
-18 \\
\hline
2.2 \\
-2.1 \\
\hline
.15 \\
-.15
\end{array}
$$

Solve.

1. $8\overline{)47.68}$ 2. $9\overline{)58.68}$ 3. $6\overline{)316.2}$ 4. $5\overline{)98.65}$

Write an equation. Then solve.

5. Imelda has 8.169 meters of rope. She wants to cut it into
   3 equal pieces to make jump ropes for her 3 friends. How
   long will each jump rope be?

   _____

6. Tonio has 7.47 pounds of rabbit food. He will divide it
   equally among his 9 rabbits. How much food will each
   rabbit get?

   _____

▶ Divide a Decimal by a Two-Digit Number

A company bought 38 sandwiches for a business meeting.
Each sandwich costs the same amount. The sandwiches
cost $161.12 in all. What was the price of each sandwich?

To answer this question, we have to divide the total price
among the 38 sandwiches. We round the divisor, 38, up to 40
to estimate the multipliers.

When $161 is divided into 38 parts, each part is $4. There is $9 left.	We change the $9 to 90 dimes and add the other dime. There are 91 dimes.	When we split 91 dimes into 38 parts, each part is 2 dimes. There are 15 dimes left.	We change the 15 dimes to 150 pennies and add the other 2 pennies. Now we split 152 pennies 38 ways.
$$\begin{array}{r} ^{(40)}\ \ 4 \\ 38)\overline{161.12} \\ -152\ \ \ \ \\ \hline 9\ \ \ \ \ \end{array}$$	$$\begin{array}{r} ^{(40)}\ \ 4 \\ 38)\overline{161.12} \\ -152\ \ \ \ \\ \hline 9.1\ \ \ \end{array}$$	$$\begin{array}{r} ^{(40)}\ \ 4.2 \\ 38)\overline{161.12} \\ -152\ \ \ \ \\ \hline 9.1\ \ \ \\ -7.6\ \ \\ \hline 1.5\ \ \end{array}$$	$$\begin{array}{r} ^{(40)}\ \ 4.24 \\ 38)\overline{161.12} \\ -152\ \ \ \ \\ \hline 9.1\ \ \ \\ -7.6\ \ \\ \hline 1.52 \\ -1.52 \\ \hline \end{array}$$

Solve.

7. $51)\overline{374.85}$ 8. $22)\overline{580.8}$ 9. $78)\overline{706.68}$ 10. $36)\overline{547.2}$

Write an equation. Then solve.

11. A rectangle has an area of 35.75 square meters
    and a length of 11 meters. What is its width?

    _____

12. Katsu bought 18 pounds of apples for $23.04.
    What was the price for each pound?

    _____

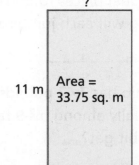

11 m | Area = 33.75 sq. m

▶ Add Zeros to the Dividend

Adding zeros at the end of a number, *after* the decimal point, does not change the value of the number. This idea can help us solve some division problems.

Eight friends bought movie tickets. The total cost for the tickets was $78. How much did each friend pay?

When the $78 is divided among 8 people, each person pays $9, and there is $6 still left to divide.	Add a decimal point and a 0. Bring down the 0 (trade $6 for 60 dimes) and continue to divide. Each person pays 7 dimes more, and there are 4 dimes left to divide.	Add another 0 after the decimal point. Bring down the 0 (trade 4 dimes for 40 pennies) and finish dividing. Each person pays 5 pennies more, for a total of $9.75.

$$\begin{array}{r} 9 \\ 8\overline{)78} \\ -72 \\ \hline 6 \end{array}$$

$$\begin{array}{r} 9.7 \\ 8\overline{)78.0} \\ -72 \\ \hline 6.0 \\ -5.6 \\ \hline .4 \end{array}$$

$$\begin{array}{r} 9.75 \\ 8\overline{)78.00} \\ -72 \\ \hline 6.0 \\ -5.6 \\ \hline .40 \\ -.40 \\ \hline \end{array}$$

13. Jun rode her bike to the bookstore and back. According to her bike's odometer, the round trip distance was 6.65 miles. She started the division at the right to figure out the one-way distance to the bookstore. Add a 0 to the end of the dividend and finish the division.

The distance to the bookstore is _____ miles.

$$\begin{array}{r} 3.32 \\ 2\overline{)6.65} \\ -6 \\ \hline 0.6 \\ -.6 \\ \hline .05 \\ -.04 \\ \hline .01 \end{array}$$

Solve.

14. $6\overline{)54.75}$ 15. $5\overline{)141.2}$ 16. $8\overline{)310}$ 17. $26\overline{)422.5}$

▶ Patterns in Division by Powers of 10

Recall that powers of 10, such as 10^1, 10^2, and 10^3 represent repeated multiplication with 10. The exponent tells you how many times to use 10 as a factor.

$10^1 = 10$ $10^2 = 10 \times 10 = 100$ $10^3 = 10 \times 10 \times 10 = 1,000$

Study the patterns in Exercises 18 and 19. Then complete Exercises 20–23.

18. $35.6 \div 10 = \underline{\ 3.56\ }$

    $35.6 \div 100 = \underline{\ 0.356\ }$

    $35.6 \div 1,000 = \underline{\ 0.0356\ }$

19. $125 \div 10^1 = \underline{\ 12.5\ }$

    $125 \div 10^2 = \underline{\ 1.25\ }$

    $125 \div 10^3 = \underline{\ 0.125\ }$

20. $50.7 \div 10^1 = \underline{\hspace{1cm}}$

    $50.7 \div 10^2 = \underline{\hspace{1cm}}$

    $50.7 \div 10^3 = \underline{\hspace{1cm}}$

21. $916.2 \div 10 = \underline{\hspace{1cm}}$

    $916.2 \div 100 = \underline{\hspace{1cm}}$

    $916.2 \div 1,000 = \underline{\hspace{1cm}}$

22. $4,076 \div 10^1 = \underline{\hspace{1cm}}$

    $4,076 \div 10^2 = \underline{\hspace{1cm}}$

    $4,076 \div 10^3 = \underline{\hspace{1cm}}$

23. $7.8 \div 10^1 = \underline{\hspace{1cm}}$

    $7.8 \div 10^2 = \underline{\hspace{1cm}}$

    $7.8 \div 10^3 = \underline{\hspace{1cm}}$

24. Complete these statements to summarize your work in Exercises 18–23.

    a. Dividing a number by 10^1, or 10, shifts the digits to the right _____ place(s).

    b. Dividing a number by 10^2, or 100, shifts the digits to the right _____ place(s).

    c. Dividing a number by 10^3, or 1,000, shifts the digits to the right _____ place(s).

▶ Patterns Relating Multiplication and Division

Use the multiplication problem to help you solve the division problem.

25. $32 \div 8 = \underline{\hspace{1cm}}$

    $8 \times \underline{\hspace{1cm}} = 32$

26. $3.2 \div 8 = \underline{\hspace{1cm}}$

    $8 \times \underline{\hspace{1cm}} = 3.2$

27. $0.32 \div 8 = \underline{\hspace{1cm}}$

    $8 \times \underline{\hspace{1cm}} = 0.32$

28. $0.032 \div 8 = \underline{\hspace{1cm}}$

    $8 \times \underline{\hspace{1cm}} = 0.032$

Solve by using mental math.

29. $6.3 \div 9 = \underline{\hspace{1cm}}$

30. $0.15 \div 3 = \underline{\hspace{1cm}}$

31. $4.8 \div 6 = \underline{\hspace{1cm}}$

Divide Decimal Numbers by Whole Numbers

▶ Use Money to See Shift Patterns

Jordan earns $243 a week. The money is shown here.

Jordan's Earnings in Dollars

$ _____ _____ _____ 2 4 3

┌─────────┐
│   ÷ 1   │
└─────────┘

┌───────────────────┐
│ $243 ÷ 1 = $243   │
└───────────────────┘

Answer each question about how much Jordan earns in coins.

1. How many dimes ($0.10) does he earn?

_____

2. What happens to each dollar? Why?

_____

_____

3. What happens to the number showing Jordan's earnings? Why?

_____

_____

4. When you divide by 0.1, does each digit shift right or left? Why?

_____

_____

5. How many places does each digit shift? Why?

_____

_____

Jordan's Earnings in Dimes

_____ _____ 2 , 4 3 0

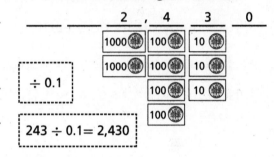

┌─────────┐
│ ÷ 0.1 │
└─────────┘

┌───────────────────────┐
│ 243 ÷ 0.1 = 2,430   │
└───────────────────────┘

▶ Use Money to See Shift Patterns (continued)

6. How many pennies ($0.01) does he earn?

_____

7. What happens to each dollar?

_____

8. What happens to the number showing Jordan's earnings?

_____

Jordan's Earnings in Pennies

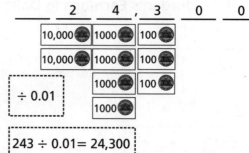

9. When you divide by 0.01, does each digit shift right or left? Why?

_____

10. How many places does each digit shift? Why?

_____

11. How many tenths of a cent ($0.001) does he earn?

_____

12. What happens to each dollar?

_____

Jordan's Earnings in Tenths of a Cent

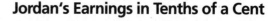
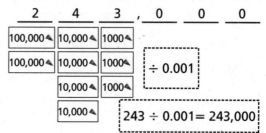

13. What happens to the number showing Jordan's earnings? Why?

_____

14. When you divide by 0.001, does each digit shift right or left? Why?

_____

15. How many places does each digit shift? Why?

_____

► Relate Decimal Division to Multiplication

Solve.

16. Mrs. Moreno made 1 liter of grape jelly. She will pour it into jars that each hold 0.1 liter. How many jars will she need?

Think: How many tenths are there in 1 whole? _____

Complete the equation: $1 \div 0.1 =$ _____.

This answer is the same as $1 \times$ _____.

17. Mr. Moreno made 2 liters of spaghetti sauce. He will pour it into jars that each hold 0.1 liter. How many jars will he need?

Think: How many tenths are there in 1 whole? _____

How many tenths are there in 2 wholes? _____

Complete the equation: $2 \div 0.1 =$ _____.

This answer is the same as $2 \times$ _____.

18. The Morenos made a kiloliter of fruit punch for a large party. They will pour it into punch bowls that each hold 0.01 kiloliter. How many bowls will they need?

Think: How many hundredths are there in 1 whole? _____

Complete the equation: $1 \div 0.01 =$ _____.

This answer is the same as $1 \times$ _____.

19. When we divide a number by a decimal number less than one, why is the quotient greater than the original number?

_____

_____

_____

_____

▶ What's the Error?

Dear Math Students,

I was absent today. My friend told me we learned to divide by 0.1 and 0.01. She said that when you divide by 0.1, the digits shift one place, and when you divide by 0.01, they shift two places. Here are two problems from my homework.

$45 \div 0.1 = 4.5$ $45 \div 0.01 = 0.45$

Are my answers correct? If not, can you explain what I did wrong?

Your friend,
Puzzled Penguin

20. Write a response to the Puzzled Penguin.

_____

_____

_____

▶ Change Decimal Divisors to Whole Numbers

You can use the strategy below to change a division problem with a decimal divisor to an equivalent problem with a whole number divisor.

Discuss each step used to find 6 ÷ 0.2.

Step 1: Write 6 ÷ 0.2 as a fraction. $6 \div 0.2 = \frac{6}{0.2}$

Step 2: Make an equivalent fraction with a whole
number divisor by multiplying $\frac{6}{0.2}$ by 1 in $\frac{6}{0.2} \times 1 = \frac{6}{0.2} \times \frac{10}{10} = \frac{60}{2}$
the form of $\frac{10}{10}$. Now you can divide 60 by 2.

21. Why is the answer to 60 ÷ 2 the same as the answer to 6 ÷ 0.2?

_____

_____

© Houghton Mifflin Harcourt Publishing Company

▶ Change Decimal Divisors to Whole Numbers (continued)

You can use the strategy of multiplying both numbers by 10 even when a division problem is given in long division format.

Step 1: Put a decimal point after the whole number.

$0.2\overline{)6.}$

Step 2: Multiply both numbers by 10, which shifts the digits one place left. Show this by moving the decimal point one place right. Add zeros if necessary.

$0.2\overline{)6.0}$

Step 3: Instead of drawing arrows, you can make little marks called carets (^) to show where you put the "new" decimal points. Now divide 60 by 2.

$0.2_\wedge\overline{)6.0_\wedge}$ quotient 3 0.

22. Why does moving both decimal points the same number of places give us the same answer?

_____

_____

Answer each question to describe how to find 6 ÷ 0.02 and 6 ÷ 0.002.

23. Suppose you want to find 6 ÷ 0.02.

By what number can you multiply 0.02 to get a whole number? _____

Describe and show how to move the decimal points to solve 6 ÷ 0.02 by long division. $0.02\overline{)6.}$

_____

24. Suppose you want to find 6 ÷ 0.002.

By what number can you multiply 0.002 to get a whole number? _____

Describe and show how to move the decimal points to solve 6 ÷ 0.002. $0.002\overline{)6.}$

_____

▶ Practice Dividing by Decimals

Solve.

25. $0.5 \overline{)45}$ 26. $0.07 \overline{)56}$ 27. $0.8 \overline{)496}$ 28. $0.65 \overline{)910}$

29. $0.12 \overline{)60}$ 30. $0.004 \overline{)16}$ 31. $0.9 \overline{)468}$ 32. $0.75 \overline{)270}$

33. $0.3 \overline{)96}$ 34. $0.06 \overline{)42}$ 35. $0.072 \overline{)216}$ 36. $2.4 \overline{)192}$

Solve.

Show your work.

37. A dime weighs about 0.08 ounce. Jake has a pound (16 ounces) of dimes. About how many dimes does he have?

_____

38. A quarter weighs about 0.2 ounce. Naoki has 2 pounds (32 ounces) of quarters. About how many quarters does he have?

_____

39. A dime is about 0.14 centimeter thick. Zeynep made a stack of dimes 35 centimeters high. About how many dimes did she use?

_____

40. A newborn mouse weighs about 0.25 ounce. A newborn cat weighs about 4 ounces. A newborn cat weighs how many times as much as a newborn mouse?

_____

▶ Use Money to See Shift Patterns

It costs \$0.312 (31 cents and $\frac{2}{10}$ cent) to make one Cat's Eye Marble. The money is shown here.

Cost of a Cat's Eye Marble

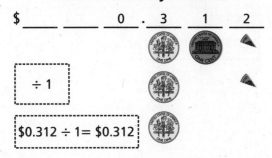

Answer each question about the different coins.

1. How many dimes (\$0.10) does it cost to make one Cat's Eye Marble?

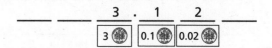

_____

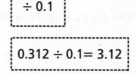

2. What happens to the number that shows the cost?

_____

3. When you divide by 0.1, does each digit shift to the right or left? Why?

_____

_____

4. How many places does each digit shift? Why?

_____

_____

▶ Use Money to See Shift Patterns (continued)

5. How many pennies ($0.01) does it cost to make one Cat's Eye Marble?

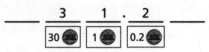

_____ 3   1 . 2 ____ ____

$\div 0.01$

_____

6. What happens to the number that shows the cost?

$0.312 \div 0.01 = 31.2$

_____

7. When you divide by 0.01, does each digit shift to the right or left? Why?

_____

8. How many places does each digit shift? Why?

_____

9. How many tenths of a cent ($0.001) does it cost to make one Cat's Eye Marble?

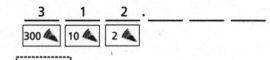

3   1   2 . ____ ____ ____

$\div 0.001$

_____

10. What happens to the number that shows the cost?

$0.312 \div 0.001 = 312$

_____

11. When you divide by 0.001, does each digit shift to the right or left? How many places? Why?

_____

12. Are the shift patterns for dividing by 0.1, 0.01, and 0.001 the same when the product (dividend) is a decimal number as when the product (dividend) is a whole number? Why or why not?

_____

_____

► Change Decimal Divisors to Whole Numbers

To divide a decimal by a decimal, use the same strategy
you used when you divided a whole number by a decimal.

Discuss each step used to find 0.06 ÷ 0.2.

Step 1: Write 0.06 ÷ 0.2 as a fraction.

$$0.06 \div 0.2 = \frac{0.06}{0.2}$$

Step 2: Make an equivalent fraction
with a whole number divisor by
multiplying $\frac{0.06}{0.2}$ by 1 in the form
of $\frac{10}{10}$. Now divide 0.6 by 2.

$$\frac{0.06}{0.2} \times 1 = \frac{0.06}{0.2} \times \frac{10}{10} = \frac{0.6}{2}$$

13. Why does 0.06 ÷ 0.2 have the same answer as 0.6 ÷ 2?

_____

_____

_____

**Here are the steps for using the strategy when the problem
is in long division form.**

Step 1: Set up the problem.

$$0.2 \overline{)0.06}$$

Step 2: Multiply both numbers by 10. This shifts
the digits one place left. Show this by
moving the decimal point one place right.

$$0.2_\wedge \overline{)0.0_\wedge 6}$$

Step 3: You don't have to draw arrows. Carets (^)
show where each "new" decimal point
belongs. Now divide 0.6 by 2.

$$0.2_\wedge \overline{)0.0_\wedge 6}^{.3}$$

14. Why does moving both decimal points the
same number of places give a problem with
the same answer as the original problem?

_____

_____

_____

▶ Change Decimal Divisors to Whole Numbers (continued)

15. How would you solve 0.06 ÷ 0.02 with long division? What number do you need to multiply both numbers by to make 0.02 a whole number?

$$0.02\overline{)0.06}$$

_____

_____

_____

16. How would you solve 0.06 ÷ 0.002 with long division? What number do you need to multiply both numbers by to make 0.002 a whole number?

$$0.002\overline{)0.06}$$

_____

_____

Solve each division problem. Show your work.

17. $0.9\overline{)7.2}$ **18.** $0.04\overline{)0.364}$ **19.** $0.6\overline{)0.372}$ **20.** $0.14\overline{)7.28}$

Write an equation. Then solve.

21. A sand and gravel company has 12.6 tons of gravel to haul today. Each truck can carry 0.9 ton of gravel. How many trucks will be needed?

_____

22. A developer is building an amusement park on a rectangular lot with an area of 1.35 square miles. The length of one side of the lot is 0.45 mile. What is the length of the other side?

?

0.45 mi   Area = 1.35 sq. mi

_____

Name   Date

▶ Divide Mentally

Use the fact that 1,715 ÷ 35 = 49 to solve each problem.

1. $35\overline{)17.15}$ 2. $35\overline{)171.5}$ 3. $0.35\overline{)0.1715}$ 4. $35\overline{)17,150}$

5. $3.5\overline{)1,715}$ 6. $0.35\overline{)1,715}$ 7. $3.5\overline{)17.15}$ 8. $0.35\overline{)1.715}$

▶ Solve Division Problems

Solve. If both numbers are whole numbers, give your answer as a whole number with a remainder.

9. $0.6\overline{)54}$ 10. $0.08\overline{)72}$ 11. $0.5\overline{)0.45}$ 12. $0.07\overline{)0.49}$

13. $0.05\overline{)34.5}$ 14. $7\overline{)395}$ 15. $0.045\overline{)41.85}$ 16. $42\overline{)4,009}$

17. $0.02\overline{)98.8}$ 18. $6\overline{)980}$ 19. $0.04\overline{)117}$ 20. $0.081\overline{)64.881}$

▶ Check for Reasonable Answers

Solve. Check that your answer is reasonable.

Show your work.

21. The Clark family is having a big lawn party. They have 196 chairs, and they want to put 8 chairs at each table. How many chairs will be left over?

_____

22. Liam needs to buy 640 eggs for a soccer breakfast. If eggs come in cartons of 18, how many cartons should he buy?

_____

23. Jacob made $507 this year delivering newspapers. If he makes the same amount monthly, how much money did he make each month?

_____

24. Johna and Pedro made a rectangular banner to display at the school volleyball game. The area of the banner is 7 square meters, and its length is 4 meters. What is the width of the banner?

_____

25. Lakisha and Raj went to an electronics store. Lakisha bought a television for $358.40. This is 28 times as much as Raj spent on a new video game. How much did Raj's video game cost?

_____

26. The Ramsey family collects and sells maple syrup. Last month they collected 57.8 liters of syrup. They will pour it into bottles that hold 0.85 liter. How many bottles will the Ramseys fill?

_____

27. Kyle spent $27.28 on postage stamps today. Each stamp cost 44 cents ($0.44). How many stamps did Kyle buy?

_____

Division Practice

► Multiply or Divide?

Read the problem. Then answer the questions.

1. A turtle walks 0.2 mile in 1 hour. How far can it walk in 0.5 hour?

   a. Do you need to multiply or divide to solve? _____

   b. Will the answer be more or less than 0.2 miles? _____

   c. What is the answer? _____

2. Gus ran 3.6 miles. He took a sip of water every 0.9 mile.
   How many sips did he take?

   a. Do you need to multiply or divide to solve? _____

   b. Will the answer be greater or less than 3.6? _____

   c. What is the answer? _____

3. Last year 135 cows on Dixie's Dairy Farm had calves.
   This year 0.6 times that many cows had calves. How many
   cows had calves this year?

   a. Do you need to multiply or divide to solve? _____

   b. Will the answer be greater or less than 135? _____

   c. What is the answer? _____

4. A box contains 1.2 pounds of cereal. A serving weighs
   0.08 pounds. How many servings are in the box?

   a. Do you need to multiply or divide to solve? _____

   b. Will the answer be greater or less than 1.2? _____

   c. What is the answer? _____

5. A rectangular patio has an area of 131.52 square meters.
   The width of the patio is 9.6 meters. What is its length?

   a. Do you need to multiply or divide to solve? _____

   b. Will the answer be greater or less than 131.52 meters? _____

   c. What is the answer? _____

▶ Results of Whole Number and Decimal Operations

Answer each question.

6. If *a* and *b* are whole numbers greater than 1, will *b* × *a* be greater than or less than *a*? Why?

_____

_____

7. If *a* is a whole number and *d* is a decimal less than 1, will *d* × *a* be greater than or less than *a*? Why?

_____

_____

8. If *a* and *b* are whole numbers greater than 1, will *a* ÷ *b* be greater than or less than *a*? Why?

_____

_____

_____

9. If *a* is a whole number and *d* is a decimal less than 1, will *a* ÷ *d* be greater than or less than *a*? Why?

_____

_____

_____

Use reasoning to compare the expressions. Write >, <, or =.
Do not compute the actual values.

10. $42 \times 356 \bigcirc 356 \div 42$

11. $0.65 \times 561 \bigcirc 561 \div 0.65$

12. $832 \div 67 \bigcirc 832 \div 0.67$

13. $738 \times 66 \bigcirc 738 \times 0.66$

14. $126 \div 0.9 \bigcirc 126 \times 0.9$

15. $3{,}500 \times 0.7 \bigcirc 3{,}500 \times 7$

16. $64 \times 0.64 \bigcirc 64 \div 0.64$

17. $5{,}602 \div 42 \bigcirc 5{,}602 \div 0.42$

▶ Make Predictions

Solve.   *Show your work.*

18. Farmer Ortigoza has 124.6 acres of land. Farmer Ruben has 0.8 times as much land as Farmer Ortigoza.

    a. Does Farmer Ruben have more or less than 124.6 acres?

    _____

    b. How many acres does Farmer Ruben have? _____

19. Mee Young has 48 meters of crepe paper. She will cut it into strips that are each 0.6 meter long.

    a. Will Mee Young get more or fewer than 48 strips?

    _____

    b. How many strips will Mee Young get? _____

20. Jenn's garden is a rectangle with length 3.5 meters and width 0.75 meters.

    a. Is the area of the garden greater or less than 3.5 square meters?

    _____

    b. What is the area of the garden? _____

21. Roberto can lift 103.5 pounds. That is 0.9 times the amount his friend Vance can lift.

    a. Can Vance lift more or less than 103.5 pounds?

    _____

    b. How many pounds can Vance lift? _____

22. The Daisy Cafe served 18 liters of hot chocolate today. Each serving was in a cup that held 0.2 liter.

    a. Did the cafe serve more or fewer than 18 cups of hot chocolate?

    _____

    b. How many cups did the cafe serve? _____

▶ Mixed Practice

Solve. Check your work.

23. 6)‾5‾.‾1‾   24. 4)‾2‾2‾.‾8‾   25. 27)‾8‾.‾9‾1‾   26. 34)‾1‾.‾5‾6‾4‾

27.　　0.4   28.　　28   29.　　0.35   30.　　78.6
　　× 0.8   　　× 0.63   　　× 94   　　× 49

31. 0.8)‾7‾.‾5‾2‾   32. 0.13)‾6‾8‾9‾   33. 0.96)‾4‾6‾0‾.‾8‾   34. 1.9)‾1‾.‾6‾3‾4‾

35.　　0.37   36.　　0.75   37.　　51.3   38.　　4.29
　　× 0.09   　　× 0.14   　　× 6.2   　　× 0.27

▶ Mixed Real World Applications

Solve. Check that your answer is reasonable.   *Show your work.*

39. Polly bought 12 beach balls for her beach party. She
    spent $23.64. How much did each beach ball cost?

_____

40. The 245 fifth graders at Miller School are going on a
    trip to the aquarium. Each van can carry 16 students.
    How many vans will be needed for the trip?

_____

41. Today Aaliyah ran 4.5 miles per hour for three fourths
    (0.75) of an hour. How far did Aaliyah run today?

_____

▶ Math and Currency

When you travel from one country to another, you sometimes need to exchange your currency for the currency used in the country you are visiting. An exchange rate is the rate at which one currency can be exchanged for another.

Currencies are usually compared to 1 U.S. dollar (1 USD) when they are exchanged. For example, 1 USD may be exchanged for 6.5 Chinese yuans or 0.95 Canadian dollars. The exact amount of the exchange often varies from day to day.

Solve.

Show your work.

1. Suppose 5 U.S. dollars (5 USD) can be exchanged for 64 Mexican pesos. What operation would be used to find the value of 1 USD in pesos?

_____

Find the value of 1 USD in pesos. 1 USD = _____ pesos

► Math and Currency (continued)

Complete the exchange rate column of the table.

Country	Currency Unit		Equivalent Amounts	Exchange Rate
2. Japan	yen		20 USD = 1,530 yen	1 USD = _____ yen
3. England	pound	£5	10 USD = 6.1 pounds	1 USD = _____ pounds
4. Germany	Euro	10 EURO	50 USD = 35 Euros	1 USD = _____ Euros

Visiting another country often means exchanging more than
1 USD for the currency of that country.

5. The exchange rate for francs, the currency of Switzerland,
   is 10 USD = 8.8 francs. At that rate, how many francs
   would be exchanged for 25 USD?

_____

6. A traveler in Latvia exchanged 5 USD for 2.6 lats. At that
   rate, what is the cost of a souvenir in lats if the cost is 3 USD?

_____

7. A tourist would like to exchange 100 USD for kuna, the
   currency of Croatia. At the rate 12 USD = 66 kuna, how
   many kuna should the tourist receive?

_____

8. The cost to visit a famous tourist attraction in Russia is
   381.25 rubles. What is the cost in USD if the exchange
   rate is 3 USD = 91.5 rubles?

_____

▶ **Vocabulary**

Choose the best term from the box. (Lesson 5-1)

1. In $240 \div 6 = 40$, the number 6 is the _____.

2. In $240 \div 6 = 40$, the number 240 is the _____.

▶ **Concepts and Skills**

3. Explain why $0.04\overline{)3.6}$ has the same answer as $4\overline{)360}$.
   (Lessons 5-7, 5-8)

   _____

   _____

   _____

   _____

4. Why does dividing 5 by a decimal less than 1 give a quotient greater than 5? (Lessons 5-7 through 5-10)

   _____

   _____

Divide. (Lesson 5-6, 5-7, 5-8)

5. $75 \div 10^1 =$ _____

   $75 \div 10^2 =$ _____

   $75 \div 10^3 =$ _____

6. $4.9 \div 10^1 =$ _____

   $4.9 \div 10^2 =$ _____

   $4.9 \div 10^3 =$ _____

7. $13 \div 0.1 =$ _____

   $13 \div 0.01 =$ _____

   $13 \div 0.001 =$ _____

8. $5.26 \div 0.1 =$ _____

   $5.26 \div 0.01 =$ _____

   $5.26 \div 0.001 =$ _____

Divide. Express remainders as whole numbers.
(Lessons 5-1 through 5-5)

9. $13\overline{)74}$

10. $43\overline{)550}$

11. $22\overline{)5,006}$

12. $7\overline{)3,535}$

Divide. (Lessons 5-6 through 5-10)

13. $6\overline{)43.2}$ 14. $8\overline{)0.48}$ 15. $34\overline{)297.5}$ 16. $13\overline{)3.38}$

17. $0.09\overline{)81}$ 18. $0.7\overline{)903}$ 19. $0.6\overline{)13.2}$ 20. $0.5\overline{)2.25}$

21. $0.32\overline{)0.8}$ 22. $0.12\overline{)1.44}$ 23. $14\overline{)171.5}$

▶ Problem Solving

Solve.

24. Monica's tomato plant is 1.26 meters tall. Sascha's tomato plant is 0.84 meters tall. The height of Monica's plant is how many times the height of Sascha's? (Lessons 5-6 through 5-11)

_____

25. **Extended Response** Use the fact that $133 \div 9 = 14$ R7 to solve Problems a and b. Explain what you do with the remainder in each case. (Lesson 5-8 through 5-11)

a. There will be 133 children attending summer camp. Nine children can sleep in each cabin. How many cabins will be needed?

_____

_____

b. Freya has $1.33. She buys as many pencils as she can for 9¢ each. How many pencils does she buy?

_____

_____

Family Letter

Dear Family,

In Unit 6 of *Math Expressions*, your child will apply the skills they have learned about operations with fractions, whole numbers, and decimals as they solve real world problems involving addition, subtraction, multiplication, and division.

A *situation equation* shows the structure of the information in a problem. A *solution equation* shows the operation that can be used to solve a problem. Your child will review situation and solution equations for addition and subtraction, and for multiplication and division. These methods of representing problems are particularly helpful when problems involve larger numbers that students cannot add, subtract, multiply, or divide mentally.

Your child will also solve multiplication and addition comparison problems and compare those types of problems, identifying how they are the same and how they are different.

Addition Comparison Problem

Terrell has 144 soccer trading cards. Manuel has 3 more cards than Terrell. How many cards does Manuel have?

Multiplication Comparison Problem

Elena has 74 stamps in her collection. Hassan has 3 times as many stamps. How many stamps does Hassan have?

Students learn that in the addition problem, they are adding 3, and multiplying by 3 in the multiplication problem.

Solving multistep problems is an important Grade 5 skill. Your child begins by solving one-step problems, then moves to two-step problems, and finally solves multistep problems which involve more than two steps. Your child will represent and use visual models and equations to find solutions for these problems.

Sincerely,
Your child's teacher

This unit includes the Common Core Standards for Mathematical Content for Operations and Algebraic Thinking, CC.5.OA.1, Numbers and Operations–in Base Ten, CC.5.NBT.5, CC.5.NBT.6, CC.5.NBT.7, Number and Operations–Fractions, CC.5.NF.1, CC.5.NF.2, CC.5.NF.3, CC.5.NF.4, CC.5.NF.4a, CC.5.NF.4b, CC.5.NF.5, CC.5.NF.5a, CC.5.NF.5b, CC.5.NF.6, CC.5.NF.7, CC.5.NF.7a, CC.5.NF.7b, CC.5.NF.7c, and all Mathematical Practices.

Estimada familia,

En la Unidad 6 de *Math Expressions*, su niño aplicará las destrezas que ha aprendido acerca de operaciones con fracciones, y números enteros y decimales, para resolver problemas de la vida cotidiana que involucren suma, resta, multiplicación y división.

Una *ecuación de situación* muestra la estructura de la información en un problema. Una *ecuación de solución* muestra la operación que se puede usar para resolver el problema. Su niño repasará ecuaciones de situación y de solución para suma y resta, y para multiplicación y división. Estos métodos de representar problemas son particularmente útiles cuando los problemas involucran números grandes que los estudiantes no pueden sumar, restar, multiplicar ni dividir mentalmente.

Su niño también resolverá problemas de comparación con multiplicación y con suma, y comparará ese tipo de problemas, identificando sus diferencias y semejanzas.

Problema de comparación con suma

Terrell tiene 144 tarjetas coleccionables de fútbol. Manuel tiene 3 tarjetas más. ¿Cuántas tarjetas tiene Manuel?

Problema de comparación con multiplicación

Elena tiene 74 estampillas en su colección. Hassan tiene el triple de estampillas. ¿Cuántas estampillas tiene Hassan?

Los estudiantes deben notar que en el problema con suma, suman 3 y en el problema con multiplicación multiplican por 3.

Resolver problemas de varios pasos es una destreza importante del 5.º grado. Su niño comenzará resolviendo problemas de un paso, luego de dos y finalmente resolverá problemas de varios pasos que tengan más de dos pasos. Usará modelos visuales y ecuaciones para representar y solucionar esos problemas.

Atentamente,
El maestro su niño

© Houghton Mifflin Harcourt Publishing Company

COMMON CORE

Esta unidad incluye los Common Core Standards for Mathematical Content for Operations and Algebraic Thinking, CC.5.OA.1, Numbers and Operations–in Base Ten, CC.5.NBT.5, CC.5.NBT.6, CC.5.NBT.7, Number and Operations–Fractions, CC.5.NF.1, CC.5.NF.2, CC.5.NF.3, CC.5.NF.4, CC.5.NF.4a, CC.5.NF.4b, CC.5.NF.5, CC.5.NF.5a, CC.5.NF.5b, CC.5.NF.6, CC.5.NF.7, CC.5.NF.7a, CC.5.NF.7b, CC.5.NF.7c, and all Mathematical Practices.

Situation and Solution Equations for Addition and Subtraction

Name _____ Date _____

VOCABULARY
situation equation
solution equation

▶ Write Equations to Solve Problems

A **situation equation** shows the structure of the information in a problem. A **solution equation** shows the operation that can be used to solve a problem.

Read the problem and answer the questions.

1. Last night, 312 people attended the early showing of a theater movie. How many people attended the late showing if the total attendance for both showings was 961 people?

   a. The number of people who attended the first showing is known. Write the number.

   _____

   b. Write a situation equation to represent the problem. Use the letter n to represent the unknown number of people.

   _____

   c. Write a solution equation to solve the problem.

   _____

   d. Solve your equation.

   _____

Write an equation to solve the problem. Draw a model if you need to.

Show your work.

2. A shopper spent $53.50 for a sweater and a T-shirt. What was the cost of the sweater if the cost of the T-shirt was $16.50?

   _____

3. Jalen had $4\frac{2}{3}$ pounds of modeling clay and used $3\frac{1}{2}$ pounds for a craft project. How many pounds of clay were not used?

   _____

4. Deborah drove 105.9 miles after stopping to rest. How many miles did she drive before the stop if she drove 231.7 miles altogether?

   _____

▶ Practice

Write an equation and use it to solve the problem.
Draw a model if you need to.

5. A car odometer showed 6,437.5 miles at the end of a trip.
   How many miles did the odometer show at the beginning
   of the trip if the car was driven 422.3 miles?

   _____

6. Enrique has two packages to mail. The weight of one
   package is $12\frac{1}{4}$ pounds. What is the weight of the second
   package if the total weight of the packages is $15\frac{1}{8}$ pounds?

   _____

7. At a track and field meet, Cody's time in a sprint event was
   17.6 seconds. What was Shaina's time if she completed the
   event in 1.08 fewer seconds?

   _____

▶ Reasonable Answers

Use your reasoning skills to complete Problems 8 and 9.

8. Suppose you were asked to add the decimals at the right,
   and you wrote 2.07 as your answer. Without using pencil and
   paper to actually add the decimals, give a reason why an
   answer of 2.07 is not reasonable.

$$\begin{array}{r} 2.65 \\ +\ 0.42 \\ \hline \end{array}$$

   _____

   _____

9. Suppose you were asked to subtract the fractions at the right,
   and you wrote $\frac{5}{6}$ as your answer. Without using pencil and
   paper to actually subtract the fractions, give a reason why an
   answer of $\frac{5}{6}$ is not reasonable.

$$\frac{1}{2} - \frac{1}{3}$$

   _____

   _____

▶ Write Equations to Solve Problems

Sometimes it is helpful to write a situation equation and a solution equation to solve a problem. Other times you may write only a solution equation.

Read the problem and answer the questions.

1. On the first day of soccer practice, $\frac{2}{5}$ of the players were wearing new shoes. The team has 20 players. How many players were wearing new shoes?

   $\frac{2}{5}$ | 20 over a box labeled n

   a. The number of players wearing new shoes is given as a fraction. Write the fraction.

   _____

   b. The number of players on the whole team is given. Write the number.

   _____

   c. You are being asked to find a fraction of a whole. Write a solution equation to represent this fact.

   _____

   d. Solve your equation.

   _____

Write an equation to solve the problem. Draw a model if you need to.

Show your work.

2. The musicians in a marching band are arranged in equal rows, with 8 musicians in each row. Altogether, the band has 104 musicians. In how many rows are the musicians marching?

   _____

   _____

3. Elena has chosen carpet that costs $4.55 per square foot for a rectangular floor that measures $12\frac{1}{2}$ feet by $14\frac{1}{2}$ feet. How many square feet of carpet is needed to cover the floor?

   _____

   _____

▶ Practice

**Write an equation and use it to solve the problem.
Draw a model if you need to.**

4. How many individual pieces of cheese, each weighing $\frac{1}{4}$ lb, can be cut from a block of cheese weighing 5 pounds?

   _____

5. An online business receives an average of 140 orders per hour. At that rate, how many orders would the business expect to receive in 24 hours?

   _____

6. A supermarket owner's cost for a 26-ounce can of coffee is $6.75. A case of coffee contains 12 cans. What profit is earned for each case sold if each can sells for $9.49?

   _____

▶ Reasonable Answers

Use your reasoning skills to complete Problems 7 and 8.

7. Suppose you were asked to multiply the numbers at the right, and you wrote 15,000 as your answer. Without using pencil and paper to actually multiply the numbers, give a reason why an answer of 15,000 is not reasonable.

   $2{,}500 \times 0.6$

   _____

   _____

8. Suppose you were asked to divide the numbers at the right, and you wrote 30 as your answer. Without using pencil and paper to actually divide the numbers, give a reason why an answer of 30 is not reasonable.

   $90 \div \frac{1}{3}$

   _____

   _____

► Write Multiplication Word Problems

**Write a word problem for the equation.
Draw a model to show the product.**

Show your work.

1. $\frac{3}{4} \cdot 2 = \frac{6}{4}$

_____

_____

_____

_____

_____

2. $\frac{5}{6} \cdot \frac{1}{3} = \frac{5}{18}$

_____

_____

_____

_____

_____

3. $\$6 \cdot 3.5 = \$21$

_____

_____

_____

_____

_____

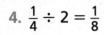

▶ Write Division Word Problems

Write a word problem for the equation.
Draw a model to show the quotient.

Show your work.

4. $\frac{1}{4} \div 2 = \frac{1}{8}$

_____

_____

_____

_____

_____

5. $3 \div \frac{1}{2} = 6$

_____

_____

_____

_____

_____

_____

6. $\$16.50 \div 3 = \$5.50$

_____

_____

_____

_____

_____

_____

▶ Use Rounding to Determine Reasonableness

Write an equation and use it to solve the problem.
Use rounding to show that your answer is reasonable.

Show your work.

1. Altogether, 91,292 people live in Waterloo and Muscatine,
   two cities in Iowa. The population of Waterloo is
   68,406 people. What is the population of Muscatine?

   Equation and answer: _____

   Estimate: _____

   _____

2. Vernon spent $229.06 for groceries, and paid for his purchase with
   five $50 bills. What amount of change should he have received?

   Equation and answer: _____

   Estimate: _____

   _____

▶ Use Estimation and Mental Math to Determine Reasonableness

Write an equation to solve the problem. Use estimation and
mental math to show that your answer is reasonable.

3. In a school gymnasium, 588 students were seated for an assembly
   in 21 equal rows. What number of students were seated in each row?

   Equation and answer: _____

   Estimate: _____

   _____

4. To get ready for her first semester of school, Jayna spent a total of $7.92
   for eight identical notebooks. What was the cost of each notebook?

   Equation and answer: _____

   Estimate: _____

   _____

► Use Benchmark Fractions to Determine Reasonableness

Write an equation and use it to solve the problem. Use benchmark fractions to verify that your answer is reasonable.

5. A $\frac{5}{8}$-inch thick paperback book is placed on top of a $\frac{15}{16}$-inch thick paperback book. What is the total thickness of books?

   Equation and answer: _____

   Estimate: _____

   _____

6. A cabinetmaker cut $\frac{7}{16}$ inch off a board that was $2\frac{7}{8}$ inches long. What is the new length of the board?

   Equation and answer: _____

   Estimate: _____

   _____

► Predict to Check for Reasonableness

Write an equation and use it to solve the problem. Use mental math to identify two whole numbers your answer should be between.

7. A $45 award will be shared equally by 6 friends. In dollars, what is each friend's share of the award?

   Equation and answer: _____

   Estimate: _____

   _____

8. Four runners competed in a 10-kilometer relay race. Each runner ran the same distance. What was that distance?

   Equation and answer: _____

   Estimate: _____

   _____

Reasonable Answers

VOCABULARY
comparison

► The Jump Rope Contest

In **comparison** problems, you compare two amounts by addition or by multiplication. Draw comparison bars when needed.

Solve.

Show your work.

1. Julia jumped 1,200 times. Samantha jumped 1,100 times. How many more jumps did Julia do?

_____

2. Ahanu jumped 1,050 times. Rolando jumped 1,080 times. How many fewer jumps did Ahanu do than Rolando?

_____

3. Altogether the Blue Team jumped 11,485 times. The Red Team did 827 more jumps than the Blue Team. How many jumps did the Red Team do?

_____

4. Altogether the Green Team jumped 10,264 times. The Yellow Team did 759 fewer jumps than the Green Team. How many jumps did the Yellow Team do?

_____

5. Ted jumped 1,300 times. He did 100 more jumps than Mario. How many jumps did Mario do?

_____

6. Isaac jumped 987 times. Carlos needs to do 195 more jumps to tie with Isaac. How many jumps has Carlos done so far?

_____

7. Altogether the fourth graders jumped 345,127 times. If the fifth graders had done 2,905 fewer jumps, there would have been a tie. How many jumps did the fifth graders do?

▶ Comparison Problems

Solve each comparison problem.

Show your work.

8. Maria scored 6 points in the basketball game. Suzanne scored 4 times as many points as Maria. How many points did Suzanne score?

_____

9. Ramon scored 10 points at the volleyball game. That was 5 times as many as David scored. How many points did David score? (Hint: Did David score more or fewer points than Ramon?)

_____

10. Ana has $15 in the bank. Her sister Benita has $\frac{1}{3}$ as much money in the bank. How much money does Benita have in the bank?

_____

11. Dana has 9 CDs. She has $\frac{1}{5}$ as many as Sonya. How many CDs does Sonya have?

_____

12. Mr. Wagner has 32 horses on his farm. He has 4 times as many horses as Mr. Cruz. How many horses does Mr. Cruz have?

_____

13. Chester has 49 CDs. Tony has $\frac{1}{7}$ as many as Chester. How many CDs does Tony have?

_____

14. A restaurant offers 18 types of pizza. A small cafe offers $\frac{1}{3}$ as many types of pizza. How many fewer types of pizza does the small cafe offer?

_____

► Model and Solve Comparison Problems

The model below represents the time a student worked on spelling (s) and math (m) homework. Use the model for Problems 1–3.

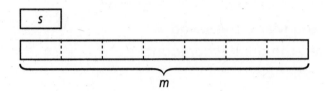

1. Write a comparison sentence that includes the words "as long as" and compares

   a. *m* to *s*. _____

   b. *s* to *m*. _____

2. Write a comparison equation that compares

   a. *m* to *s*. _____

   b. *s* to *m*. _____

3. Write a division equation that compares *s* to *m*.

   _____

Solve. Draw a model if you need to.

4. The length of an unstretched spring is 120 cm. How long (*l*) will the spring be if it is stretched to 3 times that length?

   _____

5. The length of a collapsed length fishing pole is *c*, which is $\frac{1}{8}$ times as long as its extended length. The extended length of the pole is 16 feet. What is its collapsed length?

   _____

6. A maple tree in the backyard of a home has a height of 0.75 meters. How many times as tall (*t*) is a nearby hickory tree that is 9 meters tall?

   _____

► Multiplication and Scaling

You can predict how resizing one factor will affect a product.

Solve.

7. Gina and Mario each receive a weekly allowance.
   So far this year, Gina has saved $20 and Mario has saved
   0.4 times that amount. Who has saved the greatest amount
   of money? Multiply to check your prediction.

   Prediction: _____

8. Last week Camila worked 40 hours. Sergio worked $\frac{4}{5}$ that
   length of time. Which person worked more hours last week?

   Prediction: _____

9. On a math quiz, Juan was asked to find these two products:

   $$3 \times 10.6 \qquad 2.7 \times 10.6$$

   a. Without using pencil and paper to actually find
   the products, how will the product of 3×10.6 compare
   to the product of 2.7×10.6? Explain your answer.

   _____

   b. How will the product of 2.7×10.6 compare to the
   product of 3×10.6? Explain your answer.

   _____

10. Vanessa was asked this question on a math quiz:

    *How does the value of a fraction change when both
    the numerator and the denominator of the fraction
    are multiplied by the same number?*

    Explain how Vanessa should answer the question, and include
    an example to support your explanation.

    _____

    _____

    _____

Name _____ **Date** _____

▶ Solve Comparison Problems

For each problem, draw a model and write *additive*
or *multiplicative* to identify the type of comparison.
Then write and solve an equation to solve the problem.

Show your model here.

1. Newborn baby Lila is 44.5 centimeters tall. Her older
   brother Tremaine is 4 times as tall. How tall (t) is
   Tremaine?

   Type of comparison: _____

   Equation and answer: _____

2. Brandon has $\frac{1}{4}$ cup of flour, and would like to make a
   recipe that requires $1\frac{5}{8}$ cups of flour. How many more
   cups (c) of flour are needed for the recipe?

   Type of comparison: _____

   Equation and answer: _____

3. Imani completed a 200-meter race in 25.06 seconds. Talia
   completed the same race in 1.17 fewer seconds. How
   long (l) did it take Talia to complete the race?

   Type of comparison: _____

   Equation and answer: _____

4. A high school has 1,446 students enrolled. A middle
   school has $\frac{1}{6}$ as many students enrolled as the high
   school. How many students (m) are enrolled in the
   middle school?

   Type of comparison: _____

   Equation and answer: _____

▶ Practice

Write an equation and use it to solve the problem.
Draw a model if you need to.

Show your work.

5. At the time of the 2010 Ohio census, 155,416 more people lived in Cincinnati than lived in Dayton. How many people (p) lived in Dayton if 296,943 people lived in Cincinnati?

6. A woodworking machine decreased the thickness of a board from $\frac{3}{4}$ of an inch to $\frac{9}{16}$ of an inch. By what number of inches (i) did the thickness of the board decrease?

7. The area of Alondra's home is 9 times the area of the family room in her home. The family room has an area of 192 square feet. What is the area of Alondra's home (h)?

8. Tyler has saved $14.25 of his allowance. He would like to buy a computer game that costs $15.70 more than the amount he has saved. What is the cost (c) of the game?

9. To prepare for a test, Esmeralda studied for 40 minutes. Mallory studied for 50 minutes. How many times (t) as long as Mallory did Esmeralda study?

10. A flagpole has a height of 3.2 meters. A nearby tree has an height of 25.6 meters. When compared to the flagpole, how many times as tall (t) is the tree?

11. A school fundraiser collected $776. Sun-Woo's class collected $\frac{1}{16}$ of that amount. What amount of money (m) was collected by Sun-Woo's class?

▶ Write Equations

Write and solve an equation to find the amount of money each student spent at the school bookstore.

1. Takumi: 1 eraser for $0.59 and 6 pencils for $0.15 each

   Equation: _____

   Answer: _____

2. Jasmine: 8 book covers for $0.90 each and 1 pen for $0.49

   Equation: _____

   Answer: _____

3. Dalton: 12 notebooks for $1.75 each and 1 marker for $1.59

   Equation: _____

   Answer: _____

4. Jimena: 1 compass for $2.50 and 6 portfolios for $1.25 each

   Equation: _____

   Answer: _____

5. Todd: 3 watercolor brushes for $2.39 each and a pencil sharpener for $0.89

   Equation: _____

   Answer: _____

▶ Solve Equations With Parentheses

Solve each equation.

6. $(5 \cdot 60) - 2 = n$ $n =$ _____

7. $2.5 + (4 \div 0.1) = b$ $b =$ _____

8. $3 \cdot \left(1\frac{1}{2} - \frac{1}{8}\right) = z$ $z =$ _____

9. $\left(2 \div \frac{1}{4}\right) - 1 = v$ $v =$ _____

10. $\left(1\frac{3}{4} \div 3\right) + \frac{1}{4} = c$ $c =$ _____

11. $10 + \left(\frac{2}{3} \cdot 6\right) = h$ $h =$ _____

12. $1.55 - (0.7 \cdot 2) = r$ $r =$ _____

13. $(0.01 \cdot 100) - 1 = w$ $w =$ _____

► Solve Two-Step Word Problems

Solve.

Show your work.

14. A suburban shopping mall has 105 rows of parking spaces with 45 spaces in each row. A special permit is required to park in 630 of those spaces. How many spaces (s) do not require a special permit?

Equation: _____ Answer: _____

15. A recipe that makes 6 servings requires $1\frac{1}{4}$ cups of flour. How much flour (f) would be needed to make the recipe for one-half the number of servings?

Equation: _____ Answer: _____

16. An apple orchard in Minnesota has 8 rows of 26 honeycrisp trees and 14 rows of 23 red delicious trees. How many honeycrisp and red delicious trees (t) are in the orchard?

Equation: _____ Answer: _____

17. An investor purchased 250 shares of stock. Calculate the investor's total cost (c) if the price per share was $18.40 and a fee of $65.75 was charged for the transaction.

Equation: _____ Answer: _____

18. An orange grove in Florida has 865 ambersweet trees and 32 rows of 40 sunstar trees. How many more (m) sunstar than ambersweet trees does the orchard have?

Equation: _____ Answer: _____

19. A manufacturing facility records the time its employees work each week in fractions of an hour.

Taliyah W. $25\frac{1}{2}$ hr   Avery S. $7\frac{3}{4}$ hr   Claire N. $39\frac{1}{4}$ hr

How many more hours (h) did Claire work than the combined hours of Taliyah and Avery?

Equation: _____ Answer: _____

► Too Much or Too Little Information

Solve each problem if possible. If a problem has too much information, identify the extra information. If a problem has too little information, describe the information that is needed to solve the problem.

Show your work.

Meiling is reading a 228-page book. Yesterday she read the first 41 pages of the book. Today she read the next 13 pages. Her goal tomorrow is to read 10 pages. How many pages of the book have not been read?

20. What information is not needed to solve the problem?

_____

21. Write the information that is needed to solve the problem. Then solve the problem.

_____

_____

The students in Mr. Westgate's class have been arranged in equal groups for an activity. There are four students in each group.

22. How many students are participating in the activity?

_____

To prepare for a math test, Kelsey studied for $\frac{1}{2}$ hr, Lila studied for $\frac{3}{4}$ hr, Ricardo studied for $\frac{1}{3}$ hr, and Marcus studied for 1 hour. Did Marcus study longer than the combined times of Ricardo and Kelsey?

23. What information is not needed to solve the problem?

_____

24. Write the information that is needed to solve the problem. Then solve the problem and explain your answer.

_____

_____

_____

▶ Practice Problem Solving

Solve each problem if possible. If a problem has too much information, identify the extra information. If a problem has too little information, describe the information that is needed to solve the problem.

25. A wallpaper border is being pasted on the walls of a rectangular room that measures 12 feet by $14\frac{1}{2}$ feet. The cost of the border is $6.50 per foot. How many feet of border is needed for the room?

_____

_____

26. Ms. Bleyleven has 11 windows in her house. The heights in centimeters of 4 windows are shown below.

    160.2 cm   163 cm   155.9 cm   158.5 cm

    How many windows in her house have a height that is a whole number of centimeters?

    _____

    _____

27. Anja has worked at her job for $6\frac{1}{2}$ years. Each year she works 48 weeks, and each week she works $37\frac{1}{2}$ hours. How many hours does Anja work each year?

    _____

    _____

28. During a driving vacation, a car was refueled 5 times. At the beginning of the vacation, the car odometer read 19,417 miles, and read 21,068 miles at the end of the vacation. How many gallons of fuel were needed to drive that number of miles?

    _____

    _____

► Solve Multistep Problems

Solve.

Show your work.

1. An investor purchased 150 shares of stock at $13.60 per share, and sold the shares later for $11.92 per share. Calculate the profit or loss of the transaction.

    a. What equation can be used to find the amount of money needed to buy (*b*) the shares?

    _____

    b. What equation can be used to find the amount of money received for selling (*s*) the shares?

    _____

    c. Does the transaction represent a profit or loss? Why?

    _____

    d. What equation can be used to calculate the loss (*l*)? Solve your equation to calculate the loss.

    _____

2. A soccer team plays 10 games each season. Last season the team scored an average of 2.5 goals per game in its first six games, and 3.25 goals per game in its final four games. How many goals (*g*) were scored by the team last season?

    _____

3. The charge for an automobile repair was $328.50 for parts and $64 per hour for labor. The repair took $3\frac{3}{4}$ hours. What was the total cost (*c*) of the repair?

    _____

4. An auditorium has 215 rows of seats with 35 seats in each row. A reservation is required to sit in the first 6 seats of 75 rows. How many seats (*s*) do not require a reservation?

    _____

Solve.   *Show your work.*

5. At the school bookstore, Dakota purchased a notebook for $3.75, 6 pencils for $0.20 each, and 2 pens for $1.19 each. By what amount (*a*) was cost of the pens greater than the cost of the pencils?

_____

6. A grocery store charges $4.75 for a 26-ounce jar of peanut butter. A case of peanut butter contains 24 jars. What profit (*p*) is earned for selling 3 cases of peanut butter if the store's cost for the 3 cases is $165.90?

_____

7. This week an employee is scheduled to work $7\frac{1}{2}$ hours each day Monday through Friday, and 2 hours on Saturday morning. If the employee's goal is to work 40 hours, how many additional hours (*h*) must be worked?

_____

8. Ryan went shopping and purchased two shirts for $16 each, and a pair of sneakers that cost $2\frac{1}{2}$ times as much as a shirt. What amount of money (*m*) did Ryan spend?

_____

9. At home last night, Reza spent 35 minutes doing homework, which is 10 more minutes than Colette. Katerina worked twice as long as Colette, but 5 fewer minutes than Orvis. How long (*l*) did Orvis spend doing homework last night?

_____

10. At closing time, 55 adults and 89 students are waiting in line to ride an amusement park roller coaster. The capacity of the coaster is 38 riders. How many trips (*t*) must the coaster make to give all of the people in line a ride? How many people will be on the last trip of the day?

_____

▶ Practice Problem Solving

Solve each problem.   *Show your work.*

1. Four college roommates drove 1,050 miles to Florida for spring break. Xavier drove 300 more miles than Yuri, and Yuri drove 200 more miles than Zack, who drove 60 miles. How many miles did Walter (*w*) drive?

   a. How many miles did Zack drive?   _____

   b. What expression represents the miles Yuri drove?   _____

   c. What expression represents the miles Xavier drove? _____

   d. The number of miles Walter (*w*) drove is the number of miles Zack, Yuri, and Xavier drove subtracted from the number of miles the friends drove altogether. Write an equation to represent this fact.

   _____

   e. How many miles did Walter drive?   _____

2. Sasha earns $8 per hour working at her grandparents' farm. During July, she worked $39\frac{1}{2}$ hours at the farm, and earned $47 babysitting. How many more dollars (*d*) does Sasha need to earn to buy a gadget that costs $399?

   _____

3. Anya, Jose, Cali, and Stephan walk for exercise. Anya's route is $2\frac{1}{4}$ kilometers long. Jose's route is $1\frac{1}{2}$ fewer km. Cali's route is $1\frac{1}{2}$ times as long as Jose's route, and 2 fewer km than Stephan's route. What distance (*d*) is Stephan's route?

   _____

4. A $750 gift was shared equally by 5 people. After spending $90 of her share, Clarissa divided the amount remaining into 2 equal parts. What amount of money does each part (*p*) represent?

   _____

Solve each problem.

Show your work.

5. Chloe purchased a sweater that cost $24, and a shirt that cost $\frac{5}{8}$ times as much as the sweater. What amount of change (c) did Chloe receive if she gave the clerk $50?

_____

6. Matti has 1 more pencil than Chang-Lin. Renaldo has 3 times as many pencils as Chang-Lin, and 1 more than Jorge. Jorge has 5 pencils. How many pencils (p) does Matti have?

_____

7. Six teachers, seventy-eight students, and ten parents are boarding buses for a school field trip. Each bus can carry 32 passengers. If the passengers board each bus until it is full, how many passengers (p) will be on the bus that is not full?

_____

► What's the Error?

Dear Math Students,

I was asked to find the amount of change (c) a shopper would receive from $40 after purchasing a pair of jeans for $28 and a pair of socks that cost $\frac{1}{4}$ as much as the jeans. I used the solution equation $c = 40 - 28 - (28 \div \frac{1}{4})$ to solve the problem.

The equation did not give me a sensible answer. Can you tell me what I did wrong?

Your friend,
Puzzled Penguin

8. Write a response to Puzzled Penguin.

_____

_____

_____

Practice Problem Solving

▶ Math and Gymnastics

In a gymnastics competition, gymnasts compete in events such as the balance beam, parallel bars, vault, and floor exercise.

Leigh earned the following scores from the judges for her balance beam routine.

| 9.20 | 9.30 | 9.20 | 9.30 | 9.20 | 9.00 |

Follow these steps to find Leigh's final score.

1. Order the scores from least to greatest.

   _____

2. Cross off the lowest score and the highest score.

   _____

3. Find the average of the remaining scores by adding the scores and dividing the sum by 4.

   _____

4. Calculate Leigh's final score by adding 7.0 (the difficulty rating of her routine) to the average you found in Exercise 3.

   _____

The judges' scores for Olivia's balance beam routine are shown below.

| 9.40 | 9.40 | 9.50 | 9.50 | 9.40 | 9.40 |

5. Calculate Olivia's average score by following the steps described in Exercises 1–3 above.

   _____

   _____

6. Calculate Olivia's final score by adding 6.6 (the difficulty of her routine) to the average you found in Exercise 5.

   _____

▶ Math and Diving

In diving competitions, divers compete in springboard and platform events.

Follow these steps to find the total score for a dive.

▶ Order the judges' scores from least to greatest.

▶ Cross off the lowest score and the highest score.

▶ Find the sum of the remaining scores.

▶ Multiply the sum by the difficulty of the dive.

7. Suppose a diver earned the following scores from judges on his first of five platform dives.

    9.5   10.0   9.0   10.0   10.0

    a. In the space at the right, sketch a bar graph to display the scores.

    b. The difficulty of the dive was 3.8. Follow the steps above to calculate the total score for the dive.

    _____

8. The table below shows the scores the diver received from the judges for his four remaining dives.

Dive	Scores	Difficulty
2	9.4 8.9 9.0 9.5 9.4	3.2
3	8.8 8.6 8.0 8.0 8.5	3.5
4	9.6 9.5 9.5 9.6 9.4	2.8
5	7.0 7.5 6.5 7.5 7.0	3.0

For each dive, follow the steps above to calculate the dive's total score.

    a. Dive 2 total score: _____   b. Dive 3 total score: _____

    c. Dive 4 total score: _____   d. Dive 5 total score: _____

9. How many points altogether were scored on the five dives?

    _____

Focus on Mathematical Practices

▶ Vocabulary

Choose the best term from the box.

1. A _____ shows the structure of the information in a problem. (Lessons 6-1, 6-2)

2. A _____ shows the operation that can be used to solve a problem. (Lessons 6-1, 6-2)

▶ Concepts and Skills

3. Explain how you can predict the size of the product for the multiplication 0.25 × 50. (Lesson 6-6)

_____

_____

_____

4. Write a word problem for $\frac{3}{4} \cdot \frac{1}{2} = \frac{3}{8}$ and model the product. (Lesson 6-3)

_____

_____

_____

_____

_____

▶ Problem Solving

Solve the problem. Explain how you know your answer is reasonable.

5. In a school gymnasium, 340 students were seated for an assembly in 17 equal rows. How many students were seated in each row? (Lesson 6-4)

Equation and answer: _____

Estimate: _____

_____

Write an equation and use it to solve the problem.

6. Jacqueline is mailing two boxes to a friend. The first box weighs $1\frac{3}{4}$ lb. The total weight of the boxes is $4\frac{3}{8}$ lb. What is the weight (w) of the second box? (Lesson 6-1)

_____

7. A theater has 25 seats in each row. When the theater is full, it holds 875 people. How many rows of seats are there? (Lesson 6-2)

_____

Solve.

8. To prepare for a final exam, Corine studied for $2\frac{1}{2}$ hours. Levon studied for $\frac{2}{3}$ as long as Corine. How long did Levon study? (Lessons 6-5 to 6-7)

_____

9. An investor purchased 75 shares of stock at $42.80 per share, and 6 months later sold the shares for $47.15 per share. The $20 stockbroker fee will not be charged for this sale. Calculate the total profit or loss of the transaction. (Lessons 6-8 to 6-11)

_____

10. **Extended Response** A company paid $9,000 for the rights to a software program. The payment was shared by ten friends. Eight friends each received equal amounts, and two friends each received double that amount. (Lessons 6-8 to 6-11)

a. What amount of money was each of the eight friends' share of the payment?

_____

b. What amount did each of the other two friends receive?

_____

Family Letter

Dear Family,

In our math class, we are studying algebra and operations. Your child will explore simplifying expressions using the Order of Operations.

Your child will generate ordered pairs and use the first quadrant of the coordinate plane to graph the *x*- and *y*-coordinates. An example is shown below.

x	1	2	3	4
y	4	8	12	16

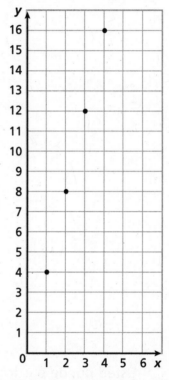

You can be an active part of your child's learning by asking your child to provide answers or examples for the following questions:

- What algebraic expression describes, "4 more than the product of 2 and *c*?"
- Generate the first five terms of a pattern with the rule *Add 5*.
- For the ordered pair (4, 6), which is the *x*-coordinate and which is the *y*-coordinate?

Sincerely,
Your child's teacher

© Houghton Mifflin Harcourt Publishing Company

COMMON CORE This unit includes the Common Core Standards for Mathematical Content for Operations & Algebraic Thinking, 5.OA.1, 5.OA.2, 5.OA.3, Geometry 5.G.1, 5.G.2, and all Mathematical Practices.

Estimada familia:

En nuestra clase de matemáticas, estamos estudiando álgebra y operaciones. Su niño aprenderá cómo simplificar expresiones usando el Orden de las operaciones.

Su niño generará pares ordenados y usará el primer cuadrante del plano de coordenadas para hacer una gráfica de la coordenada *x*- y de la coordenada *y*-. Abajo se muestra un ejemplo.

x	1	2	3	4
y	4	8	12	16

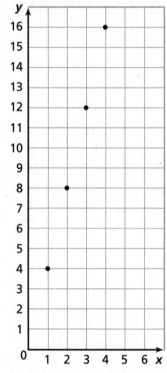

Usted puede participar activamente en el aprendizaje de su niño, pidiéndole que responda las siguientes preguntas:

- ¿Qué expresión algebraica describe "4 más que el producto de 2 por *c*"?

- Genera los primeros cinco términos de un patrón, usando la regla *"Suma 5"*.

- Para el par ordenado (4, 6), ¿cuál es la coordenada *x* y cuál es la coordenada *y*?

Atentamente,
El maestro de su niño

COMMON CORE   Esta unidad incluye los Common Core Standards for Mathematical Content for Operations & Algebraic Thinking, 5.OA.1, 5.OA.2, 5.OA.3, Geometry 5.G.1, 5.G.2, and all Mathematical Practices.

Read and Write Expressions

▶ Simple Expressions

Below are some **expressions**. Expressions do not have equal signs.

$$\frac{1}{2} + \frac{2}{3} \qquad 24 \div 3 \qquad 5 \cdot (6 - 2) \qquad 6 + n \qquad 12 - 10 \times 0.4$$

Expressions use numbers and symbols to "express" computations.

Expression	Computation in Words
$3.5 + 6.3$	Add 3.5 and 6.3.
$10 - 2$	Subtract 2 from 10.
$\frac{1}{2} \cdot p$	Multiply p by $\frac{1}{2}$.
$14 \div 4$	Divide 14 by 4.

There is more than one way to say some of the computations above. For example, for $3.5 + 6.3$, you also could say, "Find the sum of 3.5 and 6.3."

1. What is another way to say $\frac{1}{2} \cdot p$?

_____

Write the computation in words.

2. $7.5 - 2.25$ _____

3. $b + 9$ _____

4. $\frac{3}{4} \cdot 8 \cdot \frac{1}{2}$ _____

5. $1.6 \div 0.2$ _____

Write an expression for the words.

6. Find the product of 12 and 0.1. _____

7. Subtract $\frac{2}{3}$ from $3\frac{1}{2}$. _____

8. Add 14 and t. _____

9. Divide p by q. _____

► Expressions with More than One Operation

When you read and write expressions with more than
one operation, think about the **Order of Operations**.

$11 \cdot 15 + 3$	Multiply 11 and 15 and then add 3.
$11 \cdot (15 + 3)$	Add 15 and 3 and then multiply by 11.

Order of Operations

Step 1 Perform operations inside parentheses.

Step 2 Multiply and divide from left to right.

Step 3 Add and subtract from left to right.

10. Consider the expression $12 \div (5 + 2)$.

   a. Which operation is done first, division or addition?

   _____

   b. Write the computation in words.

   _____

11. Consider the expression $12 \div 5 + 2$.

   a. Which operation is done first, division or addition?

   _____

   b. Write the computation in words.

   _____

Write the computation in words. Think about the Order of Operations.

12. $3.5 - (2.1 + 1.2)$ _____

13. $\frac{1}{2} + \frac{3}{4} \cdot t$ _____

14. $(25 - 10) \div 5$ _____

Write an expression for the words. Think about the Order of Operations.

15. Multiply the sum of p and 3 by 0.1. _____

16. Divide 36 by 4 and then add 3. _____

17. Add the product of 2 and 5 to the product of 9 and 8.

   _____

VOCABULARY
simplify

▶ Simplify Expressions

If an expression does not have a letter, or variable, then you can **simplify** it to find its value. For example, you can simplify $15 \div 3$ to get 5.

How do you simplify an expression that has more than one operation? For example, when you simplify $12 - 3 \cdot 2$, do you subtract first or multiply first?

The Order of Operations tells us that to simplify $12 - 3 \cdot 2$, we multiply first and then subtract.

Order of Operations		
Step 1 Perform operations inside parentheses.		
Step 2 Multiply and divide from left to right.		
Step 3 Add and subtract from left to right.		

$$12 - 3 \cdot 2 = 12 - 6 \qquad \text{Multiply.}$$
$$= 6 \qquad \text{Subtract.}$$

1. Follow the Order of Operations to simplify $25 - (5 + 2) \cdot 3$.

    Step 1 Perform operations inside parentheses. _____

    Step 2 Multiply and divide from left to right. _____

    Step 3 Add and subtract from left to right. _____

Simplify. Follow the Order of Operations.

2. $5 + 16 \div 4$

3. $10 \cdot (0.3 + 0.2)$

4. $20 \div 4 + 3 \cdot 3$

5. $(\frac{5}{6} - \frac{1}{3}) \cdot 4$

6. $21 - 12 + 9 - 2$

7. $6 \times (2 + 4) \div 3$

8. $0.3 + 0.1 \cdot 5 + 0.2$

9. $18 + 9 \div 0.1$

10. $36 \div 3 \cdot 2$

▶ Grouping Symbols

Parentheses group parts of an expression together and let you know which operations to do first. Brackets, [ ], and braces, { }, are also grouping symbols. These symbols are often used when an expression has grouping symbols inside other grouping symbols.

To simplify an expression with grouping symbols inside other grouping symbols, work from the inside out.

$$12 \cdot [48 \div (4 + 4)] = 12 \cdot [48 \div 8] \quad \text{Add inside the parentheses.}$$
$$= 12 \cdot 6 \quad \text{Divide inside the brackets.}$$
$$= 72 \quad \text{Multiply.}$$

Simplify.

11. $6 \cdot (12 - 4) \div 16$

12. $(1 - \frac{2}{3}) \times (1 - \frac{2}{3})$

13. $(1.3 + 2.7) \div (2.2 - 1.7)$

14. $50 - [40 - (30 - 20)]$

15. $100 \div [(12 - 7) \cdot 2]$

16. $10 - \{8 \div [4 \div (2 \div 1)]\}$

▶ What's the Error?

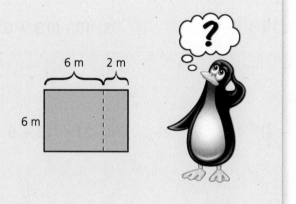

Dear Math Students,

I wrote the expression 6 • 6 + 2 for the area of the rectangle at the right. My friend said, "You forgot the parentheses." Can you explain what my friend meant?

Your friend,
Puzzled Penguin

6 m   2 m

6 m

17. Write a response to Puzzled Penguin.

_____

_____

_____

VOCABULARY
evaluate
variable

► Expressions with Variables

The expressions below contain letters, or **variables**.
A variable represents an unknown number.

$3\frac{1}{2} + x$ $n \div 0.01$ $5 \cdot (p - 2)$ $t - 6$ $4 + 10 \times w$

To **evaluate** an expression, substitute a value for the
variable and then use the Order of Operations to
simplify.

Evaluate $5 \cdot (p - 2)$ for $p = 10$.

$5 \cdot (p - 2) = 5 \cdot (10 - 2)$	Substitute 10 for p.
$= 5 \cdot 8$	Subtract inside parentheses.
$= 40$	Multiply.

Order of Operations

Step 1 Perform operations inside parentheses.

Step 2 Multiply and divide from left to right.

Step 3 Add and subtract from left to right.

Evaluate the expression.

1. $m - 4.7$ for $m = 10$

2. $5 \div x$ for $x = \frac{1}{3}$

3. $5 + n \cdot 4$ for $n = 3$

4. $\frac{1}{5} \cdot x$ for $x = 15$

5. $7.5 \times (d - 2.5)$ for $d = 3.5$

6. $48 \div (z - 6)$ for $z = 14$

7. $10 \cdot (0.05 + q)$ for $q = 1.2$

8. $2\frac{3}{4} + d - 1\frac{1}{4} + 5\frac{1}{2}$ for $d = 1\frac{1}{2}$

9. $1,000 \cdot h$ for $h = 0.004$

10. $(t + 18) \div 5$ for $t = 17$

11. $54 \div 3 \cdot v$ for $v = 3$

12. $6 \cdot 0.01 + n \cdot 0.1$ for $n = 2$

▶ Real World Expressions

13. Four friends earned $24 by washing cars and m dollars by mowing lawns. They want to divide the total equally.

   a. Write an expression for the amount each friend gets.

   _____

   b. If they made $50 mowing lawns, how much should each friend get?

   _____

14. There are $\frac{2}{3}$ as many students in science club as in math club.

   a. If there are m students in math club, how many are in science club?

   _____

   b. If there are 27 students in math club, how many are in science club?

   _____

15. Kima's cat weighs 6 pounds more than her rabbit. Her dog weighs 3 times as much as her cat. Let r be the weight of Kima's rabbit.

   a. How much does her cat weigh?

   _____

   b. How much does her dog weigh?

   _____

   c. If Kima's rabbit weighs 5 pounds, how much do her cat and dog weigh?

   _____

16. To change a temperature from degrees Celsius to degrees Fahrenheit, multiply it by $\frac{9}{5}$ and then add 32.

   a. Let c be a temperature in degrees Celsius. Write an expression for changing c to degrees Fahrenheit.

   _____

   b. Use your expression to change 20°C to Fahrenheit degrees.

   _____

VOCABULARY
numerical pattern
term

▶ Patterns and Expressions

A **numerical pattern** is a sequence of numbers that share a relationship. Each number in a numerical pattern is a **term**. Below we show the first five terms of a pattern.

$$3, 5, 7, 9, 11, \ldots$$

The pattern above starts with 3, and then each term is two more than the previous term. You can write numerical expressions for the terms. We show two possible expressions for each term below.

3	5	7	9	11
↑	↑	↑	↑	↑

Expressions $\begin{cases} & \\ & \end{cases}$

3	$3 + 2$	$3 + 2 + 2$	$3 + 2 + 2 + 2$	$3 + 2 + 2 + 2 + 2$
3	$3 + (1 \cdot 2)$	$3 + (2 \cdot 2)$	$3 + (3 \cdot 2)$	$3 + (4 \cdot 2)$

Solve.

1. a. Write two expressions for the next term (the sixth term) in the pattern 3, 5, 7, 9, 11 . . .

   _____

   b. Write the next term. _____

2. a. Write the first five terms of a numerical pattern that begins with 5 and then adds 5.

   _____

   b. Write an expression for the sixth term of the pattern.

   _____

   c. Write the sixth term. _____

3. a. Write the first five terms of a numerical pattern that begins with 1 and then adds 9.

   _____

   b. Write an expression for the sixth term of the pattern.

   _____

   c. Write the sixth term. _____

▶ Patterns and Relationships

Solve.

4. a. Write the first five terms of a pattern that
   begins with 2, and then adds 2.

   ___ ___ ___ ___ ___

   b. Write the first five terms of a pattern that
   begins with 4, and then adds 4.

   ___ ___ ___ ___ ___

   c. Circle the corresponding pairs of terms in the patterns.
   How does each term in the top pattern compare to the
   corresponding term in the bottom pattern?

   _____

   d. How does the bottom term compare to the top term?

   _____

5. a. Write the first five terms of a pattern that
   begins with 9, and then adds 9.

   ___ ___ ___ ___ ___

   b. Write the first five terms of a pattern that
   begins with 3, and then adds 3.

   ___ ___ ___ ___ ___

   c. Circle the corresponding pairs of terms in the patterns.
   How does each term in the top pattern compare to the
   corresponding term in the bottom pattern?

   _____

   d. How does the bottom term compare to the top term?

   _____

6. a. Write the first five terms of two different patterns.

   ___ ___ ___ ___ ___

   ___ ___ ___ ___ ___

   b. Describe two different relationships that the corresponding
   terms of your patterns share.

   _____

   _____

► **Real World Patterns**

Many situations in your everyday life can be described by numerical patterns. The table below shows late fees for an overdue library book. Complete the table.

Overdue Book Late Fee					
Number of Days Late	1	2	3	4	5
Late Fee	15¢	30¢			

7. Describe the relationship between the corresponding terms.

_____

_____

Complete the table and describe the relationship between corresponding terms.

8.

Bicycles and Wheels					
Bicycles	1	2	3	4	5
Wheels	2				

_____

_____

9.

Cost of Concert Tickets					
Tickets	1	2	3	4	5
Cost in Dollars		70	105		

_____

_____

10.

Weather Relationships					
Inches of Rain	0	0.5	1	1.5	2
Inches of Snow	0	5	10		

_____

_____

▶ What's the Error?

Dear Math Students,

I was asked to predict the sixth term of the following pattern.

| 1, 2, 4, 8, 16, ... |

I know that I can predict any term of a pattern if I first identify the rule of the pattern.

I compared the first and second terms and decided that the second term is produced by adding 1.

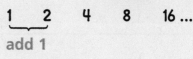

I compared the second and third terms and decided that the third term is produced by adding 2.

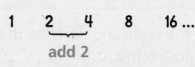

I began to recognize a pattern, which was add 1 to find the second term, add 2 to find the third term, and so on. So I decided to add 5 to find the sixth term, and I wrote 16 + 5, or 21, for my answer.

The correct answer is 32. Can you help me understand what I did wrong?

Your friend,
Puzzled Penguin

11. Write a response to Puzzled Penguin.

_____

_____

_____

_____

_____

_____

Name _____ **Date** _____

▶ Read Points

A **coordinate plane** is formed by the intersection of a horizontal number line, called the **x-axis**, and a vertical number line, called the **y-axis**.

Use the coordinate plane below to answer the questions.

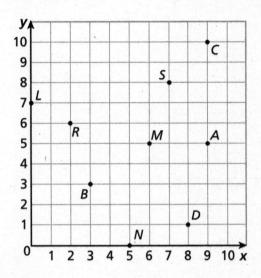

1. An **ordered pair** is used to describe the location of any point in the coordinate plane. For example, the ordered pair (9, 5) describes the location of point *A*. An ordered pair consists of two **coordinates**.

   a. The first coordinate represents distance along which axis?

   _____

   b. The second coordinate represents distance along which axis?

   _____

2. The **origin** of the coordinate plane is the point at (0, 0). Why is the origin an important point?

   _____

   _____

Write an ordered pair to represent the location of each point.

3. point *B* _____   4. point *C* _____   5. point *D* _____   6. point *L* _____

7. point *M* _____   8. point *N* _____   9. point *R* _____   10. point *S* _____

▶ Plot Points

Use the coordinate plane below to complete Exercises 11–25.

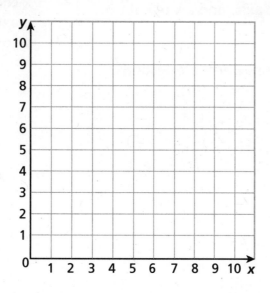

Plot and label a point at each location.

11. point *J* at (5, 4)   **12.** point *Q* at (1, 9)   **13.** point *Y* at (2, 0)

14. point *W* at (0, 4)   **15.** point *K* at (4, 5)   **16.** point *R* at (8, 3)

17. point *B* at (6, 1)   **18.** point *V* at (3, 8)   **19.** point *L* at (10, 0)

20. point *P* at (7, 10)   **21.** point *C* at (0, 6)   **22.** point *Z* at (9, 7)

On the coordinate plane above, draw an angle of the given type. The angle should have its vertex at one labeled point and sides that pass through two other labeled points. Give the name of the angle.

23. acute angle _____

24. obtuse angle _____

25. right angle _____

© Houghton Mifflin Harcourt Publishing Company

▶ Horizontal and Vertical Distance

26. Plot a point at (1, 10). Label the point *A*.
    Plot a point at (1, 7). Label the point *B*.
    Plot a point at (8, 10). Label the point *C*.
    Plot a point at (8, 7). Label the point *D*.
    Connect the points to form a quadrilateral.

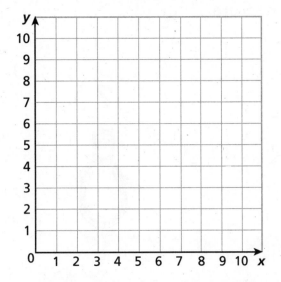

27. Explain how subtraction can be used to find the lengths of line segments *AB* and *AC*.

    _____

    _____

    _____

    _____

28. In the coordinate plane above, draw a rectangle that is not a square.

29. What ordered pairs represent the vertices of the rectangle?

    _____

30. Write a subtraction equation to represent the length of the rectangle, and write a subtraction equation to represent its width.

    _____

▶ What's the Error?

Dear Math Students,

I was asked to name the location of a fourth point that would form a square when the points are connected by line segments.

I think the point (7, 4) would form a square.

Do you think that is correct?

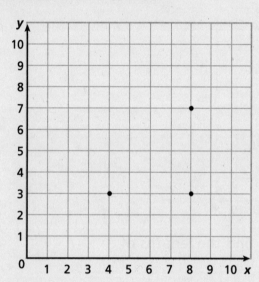

Your friend,
Puzzled Penguin

31. Write a response to Puzzled Penguin.

_____

_____

_____

_____

_____

_____

▶ Generate and Graph Ordered Pairs

Numerical patterns can be written horizontally or vertically. The *add 4* table below shows a numerical pattern in the left column and the result of adding 4 in the right column.

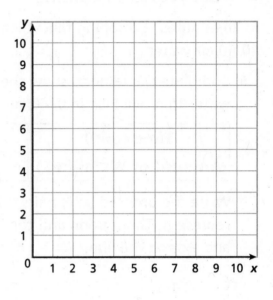

add 4	
1	5
2	
3	
4	
5	

(x, y)
(1, 5)
(___, ___)
(___, ___)
(___, ___)
(___, ___)

1. Complete the *add 4* table.

2. Complete the (x, y) table to show the ordered pairs that the *add 4* table represents.

3. Each ordered pair represents a point in the coordinate plane. Graph and connect the points.

Suppose a shrub grows at the rate shown in the table below. Use the table to complete Exercises 4 and 5.

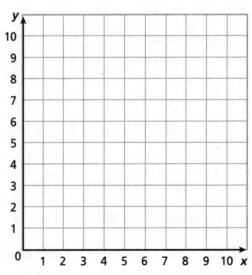

Growth of a Shrub	
Age (years)	Height (feet)
0	0
1	1
2	2
3	3
4	4

4. Write five ordered pairs that the data represent.

_____

5. Graph the ordered pairs. What does each axis of the graph represent?

_____

_____

▶ Real World Problems

**In 20 minutes, a dripping faucet leaks
10 mL of water.**

6. Complete the table to show the amount of
   water that will leak in 0, 40, and 60 minutes.

Time (min)	0	20	40	60
Amount of Water (mL)		10		

7. Write the ordered (*x*, *y*) pairs that the data
   represent. Then graph and connect the points
   and extend the line.

   (____, ____) (____, ____) (____, ____) (____, ____)

8. What amount of water would you expect to
   leak in 90 minutes? Explain your answer.

   _____

   _____

   _____

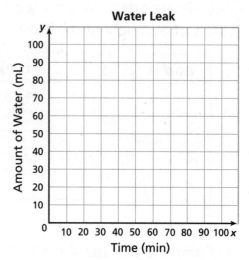

Water Leak

**The graph represents an automobile traveling
at a constant speed.**

9. The points on the graph represent four
   ordered (*x*, *y*) pairs. Write the ordered pairs.

   (____, ____) (____, ____) (____, ____) (____, ____)

10. Complete the table to show the relationship
    between time and distance.

Time (hours)	0			
Distance (miles)	0			

11. At what constant rate of speed was the
    automobile traveling? Explain how you know.

    _____

    _____

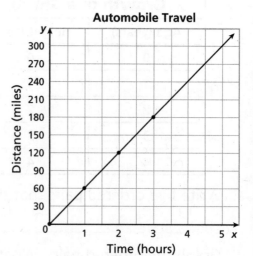

Automobile Travel

► Math and Constellations

An *astronomer* is a scientist who studies objects in space such as stars, planets, and galaxies.

Although you can see only a few thousand stars when you look into the night sky, astronomers have used special instruments to find and catalogue more than 800,000 different stars.

Constellations are patterns of a few bright stars that form pictures in the night sky. The well-known constellation Orion is shown at the right. Some people interpret the arrangement of stars as a hunter with a bow; others as a warrior with a shield.

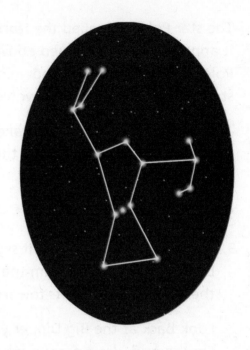

Solve.

1. The grid at the right shows the constellation Gemini. Gemini is sometimes called "The Twins." On the lines below, write the coordinates of the points that form Gemini.

   _____

   _____

   _____

   _____

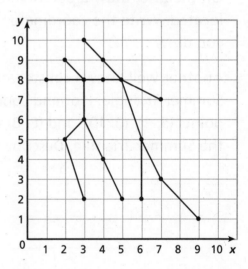

2. The points shown below form another well-known constellation that is sometimes called "The Big Dipper."

   (0, 3) (2, 4) (4, 3) (5, 2) (5, 0) (7, 0) (8, 2)

   On the grid at the right, plot the points. Then connect the points in the order in which you plotted them to form the Big Dipper.

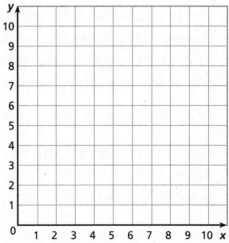

The star Polaris is called the North Star because it appears as if it is located above Earth's North Pole. Polaris is also well known because all the stars in the sky appear to revolve around it.

The picture at the right was taken by pointing a camera at Polaris and leaving the lens open for several hours.

Solve.

3. To find Polaris in the night sky, first find the Big Dipper. A ray drawn from the two stars shown at the right always points toward Polaris.

   Look back at the Big Dipper you drew for Exercise 2. On the grid, draw a point where Polaris could be located. Write the coordinates of the point you drew.

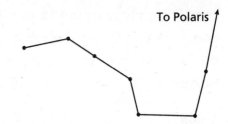

To Polaris

4. Another well known constellation is the Summer Triangle. Plot and connect the points (5, 1), (2, 10), and (8, 8) to form the Summer Triangle. Describe the triangle.

   _____

   _____

   _____

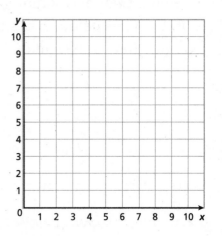

5. The points below form the constellation Bootes, which looks like a kite that has two tails. Plot the points and connect them in the order in which you plotted them.

   (7, 5) (4, 6) (2, 7) (2, 9) (5, 9) (6, 7) (7, 5)

   Form the tails of the kite by plotting points at (5, 3) and (8, 5). Connect each point to the point at (7, 5).

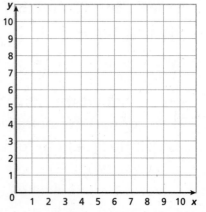

VOCABULARY
expression
coordinate plane
Order of Operations

▶ Vocabulary

Choose the best term from the box.

1. You use the _____ to simplify an expression.
   (Lessons 7-1, 7-2)

2. An _____ does not have an equal sign. (Lesson 7-1)

▶ Concepts and Skills

3. Place parentheses in the expression $4 \cdot 5 + 2 - 1$
   at the right so that it simplifies to 27.
   (Lesson 7-2)

4. Write $4.1 - 3$ using words. (Lesson 7-1) | 5. Write $8 + 7 \cdot 9$ using words. (Lesson 7-2)

   _____

6. Write an expression to represent | 7. Write an expression to represent
   multiplying the sum of 4 and 12 by 5. | dividing 10 by n and then
   (Lesson 7-2) | subtracting 2. (Lesson 7-2)

   _____

Use the Order of Operations to simplify each expression. (Lesson 7-2)

8. $16 + 4 \div 2$ _____   9. $21 - 5 \cdot 3$ _____

10. $40 \div (10 - 2)$ _____   11. $18 - (17 - 8) \div 0.5$ _____

12. $54 \div 9 + 4 \cdot 9$ _____ 13. $(0.2 + 0.8) \cdot (1 - 0.1)$ _____

Evaluate each expression. (Lesson 7-3)

14. $5 + n \cdot 4$ for $n = 1$ _____   15. $(z - 6) \div 3$ for $z = 15.9$ _____

Solve. (Lesson 7-4)

16. Write the next four terms in each pattern.

Add 8	8				
Add 4	4				

17. Describe a relationship between the corresponding pairs in the two patterns in Exercise 16.

_____

_____

▶ Problem Solving

The cost of Rosa's phone plan is $40 per month. (Lessons 7-4 through 7-7)

18. Complete the table to show Rosa's cost for 0, 1, 2, and 3 months.

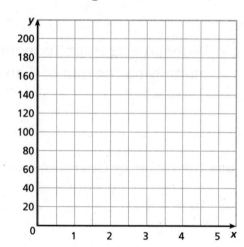

Time (months)	0	1	2	3
Cost (dollars)				

19. a. Write the (x, y) pairs that the data in Exercise 18 represent.

(__, __) (__, __) (__, __) (__, __)

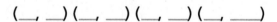

b. Graph the points from Part a. Draw a line through the points. Extend the line to the edge of the grid. Label the axes of your graph.

20. **Extended Response** Explain how you can use the pattern in the table to find Rosa's cost for 4 months. Explain how you can find this cost using the graph.

_____

_____

_____

_____

Dear Family,

Your child is learning to convert units of measurement for length, liquid volume, and weight. Liquid volume is a measure of the amount of liquid in a container. It is measured in units such as liters or quarts.

Your child will also learn about units of weight and mass. Two objects with the same volume can have very different masses—for example, iron and wood. Weight is a measure of the pull of gravity on these objects: an object made of iron weighs more than that same object made of wood. Weight is different on Earth than on the moon, but mass always stays the same.

Volume is a measure of the space that a three-dimensional figure, such as a box, occupies. This is a new topic at this grade level.

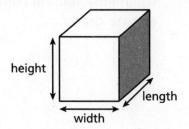

Your child will learn the underlying concepts of volume as well as multiply the three dimensions of a rectangular prism, length × width × height to find its volume. Volume is measured in cubic units, such as cubic meters or cubic feet.

Your child will also learn that attributes belonging to a category of two-dimensional figures also belong to all subcategories of that category. Students then learn to classify two-dimensional figures in a hierarchy based on properties.

If you have any questions or comments, please call or write to me.

Sincerely,
Your child's teacher

This unit includes the Common Core Standards for Mathematical Content for Number and Operations–Fractions, 5.NF.4b, Measurement and Data, 5.MD.1, 5.MD.2, 5.MD.3, 5.MD.4, 5.MD.3a, 5.MD.3b, 5.MD.5, 5.MD.5a, 5.MD.5b, 5.MD.5c, Geometry, 5.G.3, 5.G.4, and all Mathematical Practices.

Estimada familia:

Su niño está aprendiendo a convertir unidades de medida de longitud, volumen de líquidos y peso. El volumen de un líquido es la medida de la cantidad de líquido en un recipiente. Se mide en unidades tales como litros o cuartos.

Su niño también aprenderá acerca de unidades de peso y de masa. Dos objetos con el mismo volumen pueden tener masas muy diferentes, por ejemplo, el hierro y la madera. El peso es la medida de la fuerza de gravedad ejercida sobre esos objetos: un objeto de hierro pesa más que el mismo objeto hecho de madera. El peso en la Tierra es diferente que el peso en la Luna, pero la masa siempre es la misma.

El volumen es la medida del espacio que una figura tridimensional, tal como una caja, ocupa. Este es un tema nuevo en este grado.

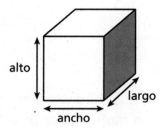

Su niño aprenderá los conceptos subyacentes de volumen, así como a multiplicar las tres medidas de un prisma rectangular: largo × ancho × alto, para hallar su volumen. El volumen se mide en unidades cúbicas, tales como metros cúbicos o pies cúbicos.

Su niño también aprenderá que los atributos que pertenecen a una categoría de figuras bidimensionales, también pertenecen a todas las subcategorías de esa categoría. Luego, los niños aprenderán a clasificar figuras bidimensionales usando una jerarquía basada en las propiedades.

Si tiene alguna pregunta o algún comentario, por favor comuníquese conmigo.

Atentamente,
El maestro de su niño

© Houghton Mifflin Harcourt Publishing Company

COMMON CORE Esta unidad incluye los Common Core Standards for Mathematical Content for Number and Operations–Fractions, 5.NF.4b, Measurement and Data, 5.MD.1, 5.MD.2, 5.MD.3, 5.MD.3a, 5.MD.3b, 5.MD.5, 5.MD.5a, 5.MD.5b, 5.MD.5c, 5.MD.4, Geometry, 5.G.3, 5.G.4, and all Mathematical Practices.

► Convert Units of Length

A meter is the basic unit of metric length. This chart shows the relationship between meters and other metric units of length.

Metric Units of Length	
1 dekameter (dam) = 10 meters	1 meter = 0.1 dekameter
1 hectometer (hm) = 100 meters	1 meter = 0.01 hectometer
1 kilometer (km) = 1,000 meters	1 meter = 0.001 kilometer
1 meter = 10 decimeters (dm)	0.1 meter = 1 decimeter
1 meter = 100 centimeters (cm)	0.01 meter = 1 centimeter
1 meter = 1,000 millimeters (mm)	0.001 meter = 1 millimeter
Example 1 Convert to a Smaller Unit	**Example 2 Convert to a Larger Unit**
2 km = _____ m	50 cm = _____ m
Multiply because we will need more of the smaller units.	Divide because we will need fewer of the larger units.
Convert kilometers to meters.	**Convert centimeters to meters.**
Multiply by 1,000 because 1,000 m = 1 km.	Divide by 100 because 100 cm = 1 m.
2 km = <u>2,000</u> m (2 × 1,000 = 2,000)	50 cm = <u>0.5</u> m (50 ÷ 100 = 0.5)

Complete.

1. 15 m = _____ mm

2. 0.36 km = _____ m

3. 2,040 mm = _____ m

4. 9.2 m = _____ cm

5. 877 cm = _____ m

6. 31 mm = _____ m

7. 2.39 m = _____ cm

8. 450 m = _____ km

9. 4,850 mm = _____ m

10. 57 m = _____ km

11. 8.6 km = _____ m

12. 41 cm = _____ m

▶ Solving Problems with Hidden Information

13. Jenny knitted a scarf that was 2.6 meters long. She made an identical scarf every month for 2 years. How many centimeters of scarf had she knitted all together by the end of 2 years?

   a. How many meters of scarf did Jenny knit in 1 month? _____

   b. For how many months did Jenny knit? _____

   c. How many scarves did she knit during that time? _____

   d. How many meters is that? _____

   e. How many centimeters of scarf did Jenny knit in 2 years? _____

Solve. Check that your answer is reasonable.   *Show your work.*

14. Natasha ran 3.1 kilometers. Tonya ran 4 meters more than half as far as Natasha. How many meters did Tonya run?

   _____

15. A European swallow flies about 11 meters in 1 second. How many kilometers could it fly in 15 minutes?

   _____

16. Allie needs 65 centimeters of fabric for the pillow she is making. The fabric costs $4.20 for a meter and the stuffing for the pillow costs 79¢. How much will it cost her to make the pillow?

   _____

17. Leon is building a square picture frame. The side of the frame is 345 millimeters long. If a meter of wood costs $7, how much will the wood he needs cost?

   _____

▶ Solving Problems with Hidden Information (continued)

Solve. Estimate to check if your answer is reasonable.   *Show your work.*

18. Pascal wants to ride his bike to and from school 3 days
    a week. His house is 2.58 kilometers from his school.
    How many meters will he ride in 7 weeks?

    _____

19. If Sabrina's hair grows 1.1 centimeters every month,
    how many meters could her hair grow over 5 years?

    _____

▶ What's the Error?

Dear Math Students,

I want to build a fence around my rectangular
garden. My garden is 675 centimeters long
and 225 centimeters wide. The fencing costs
$3 for every meter of fencing.

This is how I found the cost of the fencing.
Am I correct?

    6.75 m
  + 2.25 m $3 x 9 = $27
    9.00 m

Your friend,
Puzzled Penguin

20. Write a response to Puzzled Penguin.

    _____

    _____

    _____

    _____

Class Activity

Name _____ Date _____

▶ Multistep Problem Solving

Solve. Check that your answer is reasonable.

Show your work.

21. Mai has a piece of cloth that is 8.35 meters long. How many 15-centimeter pieces can she cut from the cloth? How much will be left over?

_____

22. On the first day of her 5-day trip, Miss Gordon drove 435 kilometers in 5.3 hours. On each of the next three days, she drove 80.78 kilometers in 65 minutes. On the fifth day, she drove 880 meters. How many kilometers did she drive in all?

_____

23. Paula's painting has a perimeter of 1.47 meters. She wants to put ribbon around the edge. If the ribbon comes in pieces that are 25 centimeters long, how many pieces of ribbon does she need to go all the way around her painting?

_____

24. Mattie is making a collar for her dog. She needs to buy some chain, a clasp, and a name tag. She wants the chain to be 40 centimeters long. One meter of chain costs $9.75. The clasp is $1.29 and the name tag is $3.43. How much will it cost to make the collar? Estimate to check if your answer is reasonable.

_____

Estimate: _____

25. Cam rode her bike 5 times as far as Dante did. Dante rode 187 meters farther than Michael did. Cam rode 15.25 kilometers. How many meters did Michael ride? Explain how you got your answer.

_____

_____

© Houghton Mifflin Harcourt Publishing Company

240 UNIT 8 LESSON 1

Convert Metric Units of Length

▶ Liquid Volume

A liter is the basic unit of metric liquid volume. This chart shows the relationship between liters and other metric units of liquid volume.

Metric Units of Liquid Volume	
1 dekaliter (daL) = 10 liters	1 liter = 0.1 dekaliter
1 hectoliter (hL) = 100 liters	1 liter = 0.01 hectoliter
1 kiloliter (kL) = 1,000 liters	1 liter = 0.001 kiloliter
1 liter = 10 deciliters (dL)	0.1 liter = 1 deciliter
1 liter = 100 centiliters (cL)	0.01 liter = 1 centiliter
1 liter = 1,000 milliliters (mL)	0.001 liter = 1 milliliter
Example 1 **Convert to a Smaller Unit**	Example 2 **Convert to a Larger Unit**
5 L = _____ mL	300 mL = _____ L
Multiply because we will need more of the smaller units.	Divide because we will need fewer of the larger units.
Convert liters to milliliters.	**Convert milliliters to liters.**
Multiply by 1,000 because 1,000 L = 1 mL.	Divide by 1,000 because 1,000 mL = 1 L.
5 L = <u>5,000</u> mL (5 × 1,000 = 5,000)	300 mL = <u>0.3</u> L (300 ÷ 1,000 = 0.3)

Complete.

1. 49 L = _____ mL

2. 5.68 kL = _____ L

3. 508 mL = _____ L

4. 8.6 L = _____ cL

5. 483 cL = _____ L

6. 227 mL = _____ L

7. 2.9 L = _____ mL

8. 4,873 L = _____ kL

9. 1,992 mL = _____ L

10. 43 L = _____ kL

11. 41 kL = _____ L

12. 58 cL = _____ L

▶ Multistep Problem Solving

Solve. Check that your answer is reasonable.

Show your work.

13. Morgan's juice glass holds 225 milliliters. If she uses
the glass to drink 8 glasses of water every day, how many
liters of water does Morgan drink during a week?

_____

14. Erin's water bottle holds 665 milliliters. Dylan is carrying
two water bottles. Each one holds 0.35 liters. Who is carrying
more water? How much more?

_____

15. Sarita is selling lemonade in 300-milliliter bottles. She made
two batches of lemonade. Each batch made 4.6 liters of
lemonade. How much will lemonade will she have left over
after filling her bottles?

_____

16. Kelly is using a bucket to fill up a barrel with water from
a well. The barrel holds 25.5 liters. The bucket holds
800 milliliters. The barrel already has 5.2 liters of water
in it. What is the least number of buckets needed
to fill the barrel?

_____

17. Tammy is making 5 batches of punch for the school's Spring
Carnival. The recipe for one batch uses 1 liter of orange juice,
550 milliliters of lemon juice, 2.6 liters of soda water, and two
750 milliliter bottles of apple cider. How much punch will she make?

_____

Metric Units of Liquid Volume

► Convert Units of Mass

A gram is the basic unit of metric mass. This chart shows the relationship between grams and other metric units of mass.

Metric Units of Mass	
1 dekagram (dag) = 10 grams	**1 gram = 0.1 dekagram**
1 hectogram (hg) = 100 grams	**1 gram = 0.01 hectogram**
1 kilogram (kg) = 1,000 grams	**1 gram = 0.001 kilogram**
1 gram = 10 decigrams (dg)	**0.1 gram = 1 decigram**
1 gram = 100 centigrams (cg)	**0.01 gram = 1 centigram**
1 gram = 1,000 milligrams (mg)	**0.001 gram = 1 milligram**
Example 1 **Convert to a Smaller Unit**	Example 2 **Convert to a Larger Unit**
5 kg = _____ g	700 mg = _____ g
Multiply because we will need more of the smaller units.	Divide because we will need fewer of the larger units.
Convert kilograms to grams.	**Convert milligrams to grams.**
Multiply by 1,000 because 1,000 g = 1 kg.	Divide by 1,000 because 1,000 mg = 1 g.
5 kg = <u>5,000</u> g (5 × 1,000 = 5,000)	700 mg = <u>0.7</u> g (700 ÷ 1,000 = 0.7)

Complete.

1. 0.003 g = _____ mg

2. 3.05 kg = _____ g

3. 25 mg = _____ g

4. 5.7 g = _____ mg

5. 294 mg = 0.294 _____

6. 0.032 g = 32 _____

7. 13.7 g = _____ mg

8. 2,441 g = _____ kg

9. 8,240 mg = _____ g

10. 75 g = 0.075 _____

11. 0.43 kg = _____ g

12. 721 mg = _____ g

► **Multistep Problem Solving**

Solve. Check that your answer is reasonable.

Show your work.

13. Hiro has 5 kilograms of potatoes and 2 kilograms of onions. He plans to use 3.25 kilograms of potatoes and 550 grams of onions for a recipe. How many total kilograms of the produce will not be used?

_____

14. A U.S. nickel has a mass of 5.00 grams. A U.S. penny has a mass of 2.50 grams. What is the mass in kilograms of the coins in a bag containing 186 nickels and 72 pennies?

_____

15. Jerry is making trail mix for his camping trip. He has 200 grams of peanuts, 350 grams of raisins, and 735 grams of pretzels. He wants to make 2 kilograms of trail mix. How many more grams of ingredients does he need to add to the mix?

_____

16. Garner is helping his mom carry in the groceries. She is carrying a bag that has a mass of 1.33 kilograms. Garner is carrying two bags. One has a mass of 580 grams and the other a mass of 790 grams. Who is carrying the more and by how much?

_____

17. Mr. Frank has 1.03 kilograms of fertilizer for the plants in his nursery. He wants every plant to get 95 mg of fertilizer 4 times each year. What is the number of plants he could fertilize with that amount? How much fertilizer will he have left over?

_____

VOCABULARY
mile (mi)

▶ Convert Units

Customary Units of Length
1 foot (ft) = 12 inches (in.)
1 yard (yd) = 3 feet = 36 inches
1 mile (mi) = 1,760 yards = 5,280 feet

Example 1 Convert to a Smaller Unit	**Example 2 Convert to a Larger Unit**
15 yd = _____ ft	48 in. = _____ ft
Multiply because we will need more of the smaller units.	Divide because we will need fewer of the larger units.
Convert yards to feet.	**Convert inches to feet.**
Multiply by 3 because 3 ft = 1 yd.	Divide by 12 because 12 in. = 1 ft.
15 yd = __45__ ft (15 × 3 = 45)	48 in. = __4__ ft (48 ÷ 12 = 4)

Complete.

1. 24 in. = _____ ft

2. 24 ft = _____ yd

3. 12 ft = _____ in.

4. _____ ft = $1\frac{1}{2}$ yd

5. _____ ft = 6 yd

6. _____ ft = $\frac{1}{2}$ mi

7. _____ yd = 3 mi

8. _____ ft = 54 in.

9. _____ yd = 144 in.

10. $2\frac{1}{2}$ yd = _____ in.

▶ Calculate Perimeter

Calculate the perimeter of each figure in feet.

11.

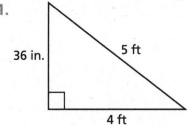

12.

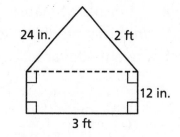

_____

_____

► Solve Multistep Problems

Solve. Check that your answer is reasonable.

Show your work.

13. Nick needs 65 yards of wire for a project. If the wire is only sold on spools which hold 6 feet of wire, how many spools will he need?

_____

14. Jessi has 9 feet of blue fabric. To finish making her costume she needs one third of that amount of red fabric. The fabric store sells fabric by the yard. How much fabric does Jessi need to buy?

_____

15. Jay runs $1\frac{1}{2}$ miles at track practice. Teddy runs the 100-yard dash, and Cadi runs half as far as Jay. How many yards do they run all together?

_____

16. Kelly is hanging shelves in her closet. She can buy shelves for $1.25 a foot. Kelly buys one 5-foot shelf and a shelf that measures 24 inches. The rest of her materials cost $90. How much change will she get it she pays with $100?

_____

17. Paula ran 24 ft with the football and then passed it 15 feet to Newt. Newt ran 70 yards for a touchdown. What was the total number of feet the ball traveled?

_____

18. Patrick bought 54 inches of material that costs $3.40 for one yard. What change did he get if he paid for the material with a twenty-dollar bill?

_____

Customary Units of Length

► Fractions and Liquid Volume

In the United States we use customary units to measure.

Customary Units of Liquid Volume						
1 gallon (gal)	=	4 quarts	=	8 pints	=	16 cups (c)
$\frac{1}{4}$ gallon	=	1 quart (qt)	=	2 pints	=	4 cups
$\frac{1}{8}$ gallon	=	$\frac{1}{2}$ quart	=	1 pint (pt)	=	2 cups

Answer with a fraction in simplest form.

1. What fraction of 1 gallon is 3 quarts?

_____

2. What fraction of 1 quart is 1 pint?

_____

3. What fraction of 1 quart is 1 cup?

_____

4. What fraction of 1 gallon is 3 pints?

_____

Example 1 Convert to a Smaller Unit	**Example 2 Convert to a Larger Unit**
12 qt = _____ cups	104 pt = _____ gal
Multiply because we will need more of the smaller units.	Divide because we will need fewer of the larger units.
Convert quarts to cups.	**Convert pints to gallons.**
Multiply by 4 because 4 cups = 1 qt.	Divide by 8 because 8 pt = 1 gal.
12 qt = __48__ cups (12 × 4 = 48)	104 pt = __13__ gal (104 ÷ 8 = 13)

Complete.

5. 20 cups = _____ qt

6. _____ pt = 2 gal

7. 15 qt = _____ cups

8. 3 cups = _____ pt

9. _____ gal = 48 qt

10. 144 cups = _____ gal

11. _____ pt = $2\frac{1}{2}$ qt

12. 23 pt = _____ cups

13. _____ qt = $1\frac{1}{2}$ gal

▶ Solve Multistep Problems

Solve. Check that your answer is reasonable.   *Show your work.*

14. A muffin recipe requires $2\frac{3}{4}$ cups of milk. What amount of milk do you need to make double the number of muffins?

_____

15. A recipe requires $\frac{3}{4}$ cup of water. Farha has a measuring cup that is marked only in ounces, but she knows that 8 ounces is equivalent to 1 cup. How many ounces of water will she add to the mixture? Explain.

_____

_____

16. A serving size for pineapple-orange punch is $\frac{1}{2}$ cup. Liam needs to make 72 servings of punch. He will use 8 pints of pineapple juice. The rest is orange juice. How many pints of orange juice does he need to make the punch?

_____

17. Melanie and Brad each drink 10 cups of water every day. Lara drinks 3 quarts of water every day. How many gallons of water do the three of them drink altogether each week?

_____

18. Angela and Ryou are painting a room. Angela has $2\frac{1}{2}$ gallons of blue paint and Ryou has half as much white paint. It will take $2\frac{3}{4}$ quarts to cover each wall. If each wall is painted only one color, how many walls will be blue and how many will be white? How much paint will be left over?

_____

_____

Customary Measures of Liquid Volume

► Fractions and Weight

Customary units of weight include ounces, pounds, and **tons**.

ounce (oz)	pound (lb)	ton (T)
1 lb = 16 oz	1 lb	1 T = 2,000 lb

1. The table below shows how to use fractions to compare ounces to pounds. Complete the table by writing each fraction in simplest form.

Ounces (oz)	1	2	4	8	12
Pounds (lb)	$\frac{1}{16}$	$\frac{1}{8}$			

Example 1 **Convert to a Smaller Unit**	Example 2 **Convert to a Larger Unit**
4 T = _____ lb	144 oz = _____ lb
Multiply because we will need more of the smaller units.	Divide because we will need fewer of the larger units.
Convert tons to pounds.	**Convert ounces to pounds.**
Multiply by 2,000 because 2,000 lb = 1 T.	Divide by 16 because 16 oz = 1 lb.
4 T = <u>8,000</u> lb (4 × 2,000 = 8,000)	144 oz = <u>9</u> lb (144 ÷ 16 = 9)

Complete.

2. 64 oz = _____ lb

3. _____ T = 10,000 lb

4. 11 T = _____ lb

5. 16 lb = _____ oz

6. _____ T = 14,000 lb

7. 160 oz = _____ lb

8. _____ oz = $5\frac{1}{4}$ lb

9. 848 oz = _____ lb

10. _____ lb = 720 oz

► Solve Multistep Problems

Solve. Check that your answer is reasonable.

11. A $\frac{1}{4}$-lb package of sunflower seeds costs 79¢. An 8-ounce package costs $1.59. Which package represents the lower cost per ounce?

_____

12. Melissa is measuring 132 oz of rice into one-pound containers. How many one-pound containers will she need to hold all of the rice? How many ounces of rice will she need to buy if she needs 10 pounds of rice?

_____

13. A casserole recipe calls for 4 ounces of cheese. Adrian wants to use $\frac{1}{2}$ of the amount of cheese in his casseroles. How many pounds of cheese does he need to make 28 casseroles with his revised recipe?

_____

14. The four elephants at the Sunnypark Zoo each eat 150 pounds of food a day. The bulk of their diet is hay, but they also eat fruits, vegetables, and pellet food. How many tons of food do the four elephants eat during the month of April?

_____

15. A cargo truck is carrying three identical boxes. The weight of each box is $2\frac{1}{2}$ tons. Explain how to use mental math to find the total weight of the boxes in pounds.

_____

_____

_____

_____

▶ Line Plots

Two number cubes, labeled 1 to 6, were tossed 30 times. This **frequency table** shows the number of times each total occurred. You can organize data on a **line plot** to make the data easier to analyze.

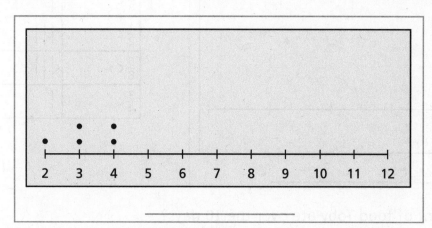

Totals for 2 cubes	Number of tosses
2	1
3	2
4	2
5	3
6	5
7	6
8	4
9	4
10	2
11	1
12	0

1. The line plot has been filled in for tosses of 2, 3, and 4. Complete the rest of the line plot.

2. Based on this sample, describe the totals that are least likely to be tossed.

   _____

3. Based on this sample, describe the totals that are most likely to be tossed.

   _____

4. Why doesn't a total of 1 appear on the line plot or in the table?

   _____

   _____

   _____

5. Explain why a total of 7 was the most likely sum tossed.

   _____

   _____

   _____

▶ Line Plots with Fractional Units

6. For 10 days, Mario measured the amount of food that his cat Toby ate each day. The amounts he recorded are shown in the table at the right. Graph the results on the line plot.

Amounts Toby Ate Each Day for 10 Days	
$\frac{1}{4}$ c	||
$\frac{3}{8}$ c	|
$\frac{1}{2}$ c	|||
$\frac{5}{8}$ c	|||
$\frac{3}{4}$ c	|

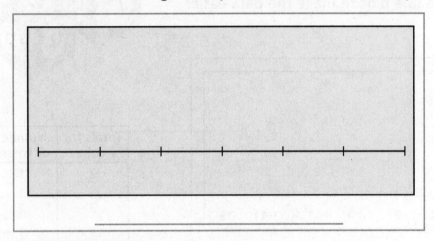

a. What is the total amount of food Toby ate over the 10 days? Explain how you got your answer.

_____

_____

b. What amount of food would Toby get if the total for 10 days was distributed evenly each day?

_____

7. Lilly bought a bag of beads of mixed sizes. She made the frequency table below showing the number of beads of each size. Make a line plot using her data. Write a question that can be solved using the line plot.

Diameter of Beads (in.)	
$\frac{1}{8}$	|||||
$\frac{1}{4}$	|||
$\frac{3}{8}$	||||
$\frac{1}{2}$	||

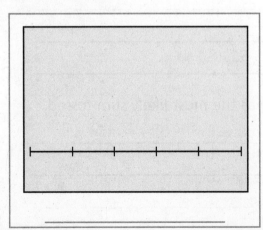

_____

_____

_____

_____

_____

_____

VOCABULARY
perimeter
area

▶ Discuss Perimeter and Area

Perimeter is the distance around a figure.

Area is the total number of square units that cover a figure.

Rectangle A

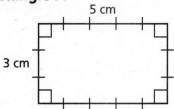

$P = 3 \text{ cm} + 5 \text{ cm} + 3 \text{ cm} + 5 \text{ cm} = 16 \text{ cm}$

Formula: _____

Rectangle B

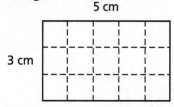

$A = 3 \text{ cm} \times 5 \text{ cm} = 15 \text{ sq cm}$

Formula: _____

▶ Discuss Fractional Side Lengths

To find the area of a rectangle with fractional side lengths, use the same method you use to find the area of a rectangle with whole-number side lengths.

Rectangle C

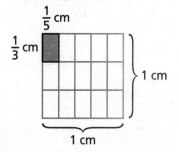

$A = 1$ of 15 equal parts

$A = \frac{1}{3} \text{ cm} \times \frac{1}{5} \text{ cm} = \frac{1}{15} \text{ sq cm}$

Rectangle D

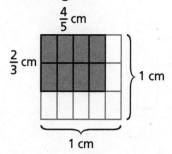

$A = $ eight $\frac{1}{15}$'s

$A = \frac{2}{3} \text{ cm} \times \frac{4}{5} \text{ cm} = \frac{8}{15} \text{ sq cm}$

Find the perimeter of each green rectangle.

1. Rectangle C: _____

2. Rectangle D: _____

3. Discuss how finding the perimeter of a rectangle with fractional side lengths is the same as and different from finding the perimeter of a rectangle with whole-number side lengths.

► **Analyze Area Models with Fractional Side Lengths**

Solve.

4. Shade and label the model to show the area of a $\frac{1}{2}$ mi by $\frac{1}{4}$ mi rectangle. Describe what your model shows and then find the area numerically.

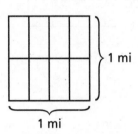

1 mi

1 mi

_____

_____

_____

_____

_____

5. Shade the model to show the area of a $\frac{1}{2}$ mi by $\frac{3}{4}$ mi rectangle. Describe what your model shows and then find the area numerically.

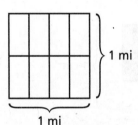

1 mi

1 mi

_____

_____

_____

_____

► **Find an Unknown Side Length**

6. What is the length of a rectangle with a width of 27 feet and an area of 918 square feet?

_____

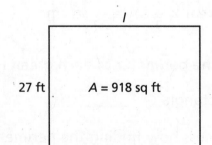

l

27 ft   *A* = 918 sq ft

► Practice with Area

Find the perimeter and the area of the rectangle.

7.
$\frac{1}{2}$ cm

$\frac{1}{2}$ cm

P = _____

A = _____

8.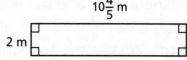
$10\frac{4}{5}$ m

2 m

P = _____

A = _____

9.
4 in.

5 in.

P = _____

A = _____

10.
$1\frac{4}{5}$ cm

$\frac{2}{3}$ cm

P = _____

A = _____

Find the side length of the rectangle.

11.
_____ m

4.8 m   A = 29.76 sq m

12.
$\frac{1}{3}$ ft

_____ ft   A = 2 sq ft

13.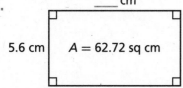
_____ cm

5.6 cm   A = 62.72 sq cm

14.
_____ yd

$\frac{1}{2}$ yd   A = 7 sq yd

▶ Solve Real World Problems

Solve.

Show Your Work.

15. Brian was tiling a patio and ran out of tiles. The width of the remaining area is $\frac{2}{3}$ yard. The length of the remaining area is 4 yards. What is the area Brian has left to tile?

_____

16. Rylee knows that the area for the face-painting station is 166 square feet. She knows that the length of the rectangular area is 12 feet. How wide is the area?

_____

17. Coby needs to know the area and perimeter of his farm property. The length of his property is $\frac{1}{12}$ mile and the width is $\frac{3}{8}$ mile. What is the area? What is the perimeter?

_____

18. The area for the dance floor is 45 square feet, and one side is 8 feet. What is the length of the other side?

_____

19. Margo wants new carpet and a new wallpaper border for her bedroom. The room is 5.4 meters long and $4\frac{7}{8}$ meters wide. About how many square yards of carpet will she need? About how many yards of wallpaper border will she need?

_____

20. Tomas has a garden with a length of 2.45 meters and a width of $\frac{5}{8}$ meters. Use benchmarks to estimate the area and perimeter of the garden.

_____

21. Laura has a rectangular piece of wood that is 7 inches by 4 inches. She wants to cover it with strips of ribbon that are $\frac{1}{4}$ inch wide. What length of ribbon does she need to cover the wood?

_____

VOCABULARY
face
edge
unit cube
volume
cubic unit

▶ Describe a Cube

Use the cube to answer the questions below.

1. How many **faces** does a cube have? _____

2. How many **edges** does a cube have? _____

Write *true* or *false* for each statement.

3. All the edges of a cube are the same length. _____

4. All the faces of a cube are the same size squares. _____

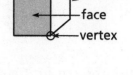

▶ Explore Volume

A **unit cube** is a cube with each edge 1 unit long. The volume of a unit cube is 1 **cubic unit**. The **volume** of an object can be measured by filling it with unit cubes without any gaps or overlaps.

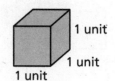

Cut out the nets. Fold each of the nets to make an open-ended prism. Fill the prisms with 1-cm cubes leaving no spaces.

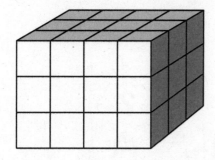

5. Number of cubes: _____

6. Volume: _____

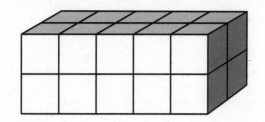

7. Number of cubes: _____

8. Volume: _____

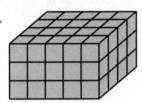
▶ Unit Cubes and Volume

Find the number of unit cubes and the volume.

9.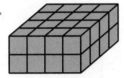

Number of unit cubes: _____

Volume: _____

10.

Number of cubes: _____

Volume: _____

11.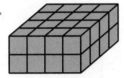

Number of unit cubes: _____

Volume: _____

12.

Number of unit cubes: _____

Volume: _____

▶ What's the Error?

Dear Math Students,

This drawing of a cube appears to have a volume of 19 cubic units but, when I built it, I used 27 cubes.
What did I do wrong?

Your Friend,
Puzzled Penguin

13. Write a response to Puzzled Penguin.

_____

_____

_____

▶ Nets for Rectangular Prisms

Cut out the nets and form the open-ended prism.

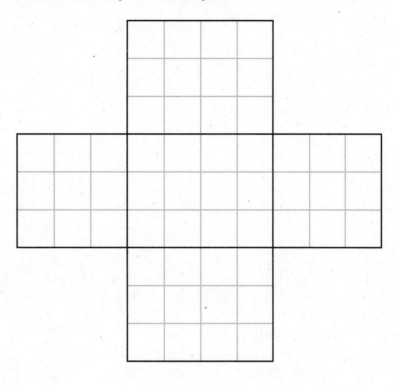

Name

Date

▶ Nets for Rectangular Prisms (continued)

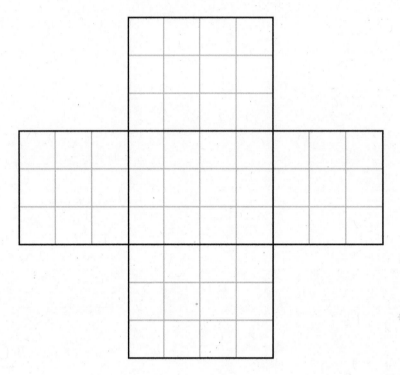

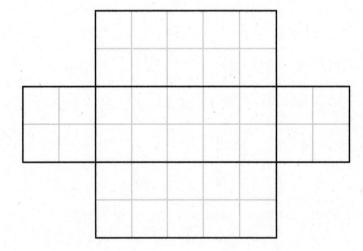

Cubic Units and Volume

VOCABULARY
rectangular prism
volume
cubic unit

▶ Explore Layers

You can use layers of cubes to build **rectangular prisms**.

Each layer of these rectangular prisms is 4 cubes by 2 cubes. How many cubes make up each prism?

1 layer
_____

2 layers	**3 layers**	**4 layers**	**5 layers**	**6 layers**
_____	_____	_____	_____	_____

The **volume** of a prism is the number of cubes needed to build the prism. Volume is recorded in **cubic units**.

Write the volume of the prism in cubic units.

1. 1 layer: $4 \times 2 \times 1 =$ _____ cubic units

2. 2 layers: $4 \times 2 \times 2 =$ _____ cubic units

3. 3 layers: $4 \times 2 \times 3 =$ _____ cubic units

4. 4 layers: $4 \times 2 \times 4 =$ _____ cubic units

5. 5 layers: $4 \times 2 \times 5 =$ _____ cubic units

6. 6 layers: $4 \times 2 \times 6 =$ _____ cubic units

Name _____   Date _____

► Calculate Volume

Complete the table.

Prism	length (*l*)	width (*w*)	height (*h*)	(length × width) × height (*l* × *w*) × *h*	volume (*V*)
7. 5 ft, 4 ft, 7 ft	7 ft	4 ft	5 ft	(7 × 4) × 5	140 cu ft
8. 10 cm, 15 cm, 6 cm					
9. 4 m, 4 m, 12 m					
10. 8 in., 4 in., 5 in.					
11. 7 cm, 10 cm, 15 cm					
12. 6 in., 6 in., 6 in.					

▶ Develop a Formula

1. What is the volume of this rectangular prism?

   _____

2. How do you find the area of a rectangle?

   _____

3. How do you find the volume of a rectangular prism?

   _____

4. How is finding volume different from finding area?

   _____

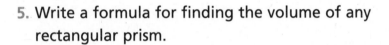

5. Write a formula for finding the volume of any rectangular prism.

   Volume = _____

6. This ice cube is shaped like a cube. Its edge lengths are 2 cm. What is the volume of this ice cube? Write a formula for finding the volume of any cube.

   _____

   _____

▶ Find an Unknown Edge

7. Raul is building a planter in the shape of a rectangular prism. It has a length of 4 feet and a height of 2 feet. How wide should it be to hold 24 cubic feet of soil? Explain how you found your answer.

   _____

   _____

   _____

   _____

▶ Practice

Write a numerical expression for the volume. Then calculate the volume.

8.
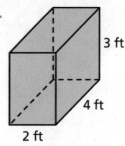

3 ft

4 ft

2 ft

9.
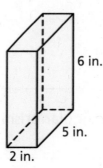

6 in.

5 in.

2 in.

10.
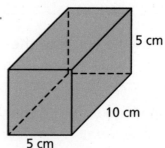

5 cm

10 cm

5 cm

Expression: _____

Expression: _____

Expression: _____

Volume: _____

Volume: _____

Volume: _____

Find the unknown dimension or volume of each rectangular prism.

11. V = 120 cu m

   l = 4 m

   w = _____

   h = 5 m

12. V = 120 cu in.

   l = _____

   w = 4 in.

   h = 3 in.

13. V = _____

   l = 7 cm

   w = 6 cm

   h = 7 cm

Write an equation. Then solve.

14. A box shaped like a rectangular prism is 2 m long, 2 m wide, and has a height of 3 m. What is the volume of the box?

_____

15. Fred's dog crate is 42 inches long, 24 inches wide, and has a height of 30 inches. What is the volume of the crate?

_____

16. The cargo hold of a truck has a height of 3 yards and is 5 yards wide. The volume of the cargo hold is listed as 240 cubic yards. What is the length of the cargo hold?

_____

VOCABULARY
length: one-dimensional
area: two-dimensional
volume: three-dimensional

▶ Compare Length, Area, and Volume

Length tells how wide, tall, or long something is.
Finding length requires one measurement.
Length is **one-dimensional** and is measured in
linear units.

Area tells how much surface a figure covers.
Finding the area of a rectangle requires two linear
measurements. Area is **two-dimensional** and is
measured in square units.

Volume tells how much space an object occupies.
Finding the volume of a rectangular prism requires three
linear measurements. Volume is **three-dimensional** and
is measured in cubic units.

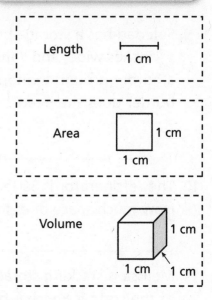

**To answer the question, tell if you need to measure for length, area,
or volume. Then write the number of measurements you need to make.**

1. How much water is in a swimming pool? _____

2. How tall are you? _____

3. How much carpet is needed for a floor? _____

4. How far is it from a doorknob to the floor? _____

5. How much sand is in a sandbox? _____

6. How much wallpaper is needed for one wall? _____

7. How long is a string? _____

8. How much space is there inside a refrigerator? _____

▶ Solve Real World Problems

Solve.

9. Soledad has a storage box. The box is $6\frac{1}{2}$ inches long, $4\frac{3}{4}$ inches wide, and 7 inches tall. She wants to run a border around the top of the box. How much border does she need?

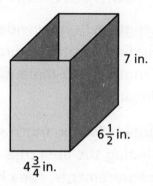

7 in.

$6\frac{1}{2}$ in.

$4\frac{3}{4}$ in.

_____

10. The refrigerator is $5\frac{2}{3}$ feet tall, $2\frac{2}{7}$ feet wide, and $2\frac{1}{4}$ feet deep. How much space does the refrigerator take up on the floor?

_____

11. Melissa is stacking storage cubes in a crate. The bottom of the crate is 8 inches by 12 inches. The volume of the crate is 768 cu inches. If a storage cube has a length of 4 inches, how many storage cubes will fit in the crate?

_____

12. Reed has a lawn mowing service and charges $1.00 for mowing 15 square yards of lawn. On Saturday he mows 5 lawns that are each $21\frac{3}{4}$ yards by 27 yards. How much money does Reed earn on Saturday?

_____

13. Parker builds a planter in the shape of a rectangular prism that is 6 feet wide, 3 feet deep, and 2 feet tall. How much soil will he need to fill it?

_____

14. A box is a rectangular prism with a square base. The volume is 972 cubic centimeters and the area of the square base is 81 square centimeters. What is the height of the box? Explain how you found your answer.

_____

Relate Length, Area, and Volume

VOCABULARY
composite

▶ Analyze a Composite Solid Figure

A **composite** solid can be made by putting together
two or more rectangular prisms. To find the volume
of such a composite solid, divide it into individual
prisms. Use the formula $V = l \cdot w \cdot h$ to find the
volume of each individual prism, and then add
the volumes to find the total volume.

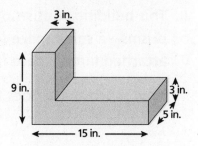

**To find the volume, you can decompose the solid into
different rectangular prisms.**

1. Find the volume of the blue rectangular prism first.

   $V = $ _____ $\times$ _____ $\times$ _____ $= $ _____ cubic inches

   $V = $ _____ $\times$ _____ $\times$ _____ $= $ _____ cubic inches

   Total volume = _____ + _____ = _____ cubic inches

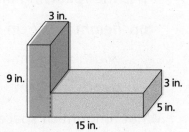

2. Find the volume of the blue rectangular prism first.

   $V = $ _____ $\times$ _____ $\times$ _____ $= $ _____ cubic inches

   $V = $ _____ $\times$ _____ $\times$ _____ $= $ _____ cubic inches

   Total volume = _____ + _____ = _____ cubic inches

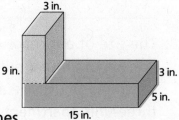

3. **Discuss** Compare your answers to Problems 1 and 2.
   What conclusion or conclusions can you make?

▶ Practice

Find the volume of each composite solid figure.

4.

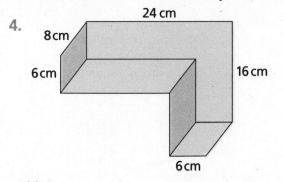

   $V = $ _____

5.

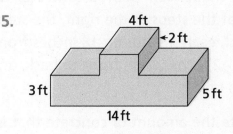

   $V = $ _____

▶ Real World Problems

6. This building consists of two rectangular prisms—a small space for offices and an attached larger space for warehouse storage.

   How much space does the building take up?

   _____

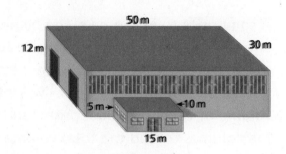

7. When Jayna's notebook computer is open, it has the following dimensions:

   top *height* = 0.7 cm   **bottom** *height* = 1.5 cm

        width = 33 cm   *width* = 33 cm

        depth = 24 cm   *depth* = 24 cm

   What amount of space does Jayna's notebook take up when it is closed?

   _____

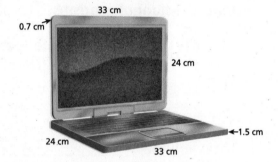

8. The size of a furnace depends on the volume of air in a building. A heating contractor must size a furnace for the three-unit apartment building shown in the sketch at the right.

   What is the volume of air in the building?

   _____

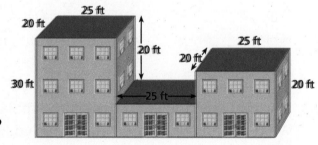

9. An in-ground swimming pool often has steps that are made from poured concrete. In the sketch of the steps at the right, the steps are identical, each measuring 18 inches from side to side, 12 inches from front to back, and 8 inches tall.

   Calculate the amount of concrete that is needed to form the steps.

   _____

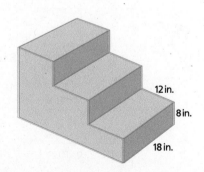

Volume of Composite Solid Figures

► Reasoning About Quadrilaterals

In Exercises 1–6, write *true* or *false*. If the statement is false, sketch a counterexample.

1. All quadrilaterals have at least one pair of parallel sides.

2. All squares have a pair of perpendicular sides.

3. A rhombus must have an acute angle.

4. All rectangles have opposite sides that are the same length.

5. All squares have opposite sides that are parallel.

6. A quadrilateral with a right angle must be a rectangle.

Sketch a shape that fits the description if possible.

7. a parallelogram with exactly two right angles

8. a trapezoid with one line of symmetry

9. a rectangle with adjacent sides that are the same length

10. a square that is not a rhombus

VOCABULARY
quadrilateral
parallelogram
trapezoid
rectangle
rhombus
square

► Classify Quadrilaterals

A **quadrilateral** is a closed shape with four straight sides. The diagram below shows how the categories of quadrilaterals are related.

11. List the letters of the shapes from Quadrilaterals A–T that belong in each category. (Many shapes belong to more than one category.) Then complete the statements.

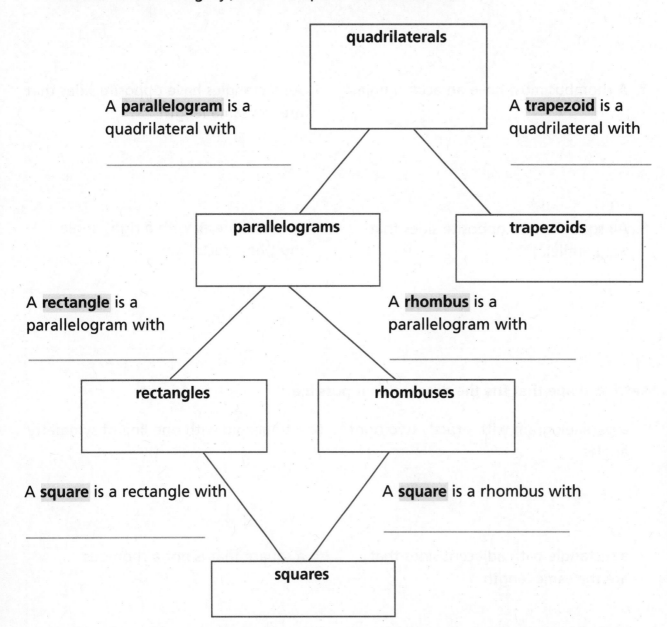

A **parallelogram** is a quadrilateral with

_____

A **trapezoid** is a quadrilateral with

_____

A **rectangle** is a parallelogram with

_____

A **rhombus** is a parallelogram with

_____

A **square** is a rectangle with

_____

A **square** is a rhombus with

_____

► Quadrilateral Cards

quadrilateral	quadrilateral	quadrilateral	quadrilateral
A	B	C	D
quadrilateral	quadrilateral	quadrilateral	quadrilateral
E	F	G	H
quadrilateral	quadrilateral	quadrilateral	quadrilateral
I	J	K	L
quadrilateral	quadrilateral	quadrilateral	quadrilateral
M	N	O	P
quadrilateral	quadrilateral	quadrilateral	quadrilateral
Q	R	S	T

▶ Reasoning About Triangles

**In Exercises 1–6, write *true* or *false*. If the statement
is false, sketch a counterexample.**

1. All isosceles triangles are also
equilateral.

2. A scalene triangle cannot have a line
of symmetry.

3. All right triangles have two acute
angles.

4. Any triangle with an obtuse angle
must be scalene.

5. All equilateral triangles are acute.

6. A scalene triangle cannot have a right
angle.

Sketch a shape that fits the description if possible.

7. an isosceles triangle with a right angle

8. a triangle with two right angles

9. a triangle with more than one line of
symmetry

10. an isosceles triangle without a line of
symmetry

VOCABULARY
acute triangle
obtuse triangle
right triangle
equilateral triangle
isosceles triangle
scalene triangle

▶ Classify Triangles

Write the letters of the shapes from Triangles A–L in the correct region of each diagram.

11. Triangles

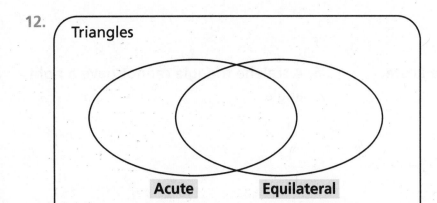

Right   **Isosceles**

12. Triangles

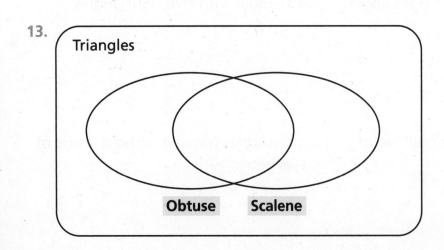

Acute   **Equilateral**

13. Triangles

Obtuse   **Scalene**

▶ Triangle Cards

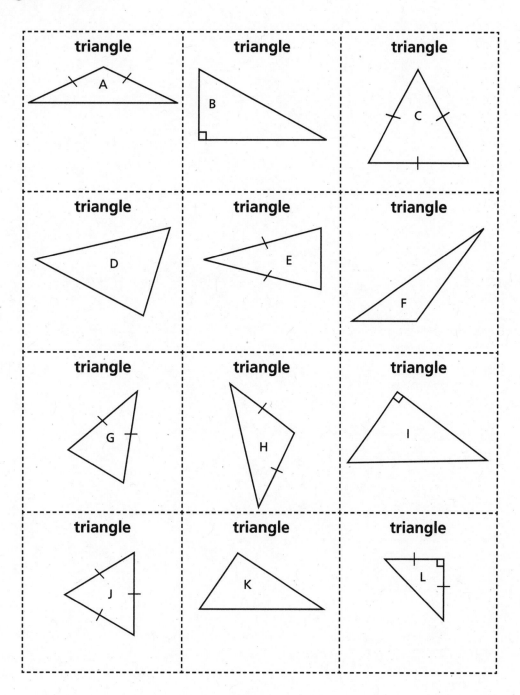

© Houghton Mifflin Harcourt Publishing Company

Attributes of Triangles

VOCABULARY
open   concave
closed   convex
polygon

▶ Two-Dimensional Shapes

Two-dimensional shapes can be made up of line segments or curves or both.

Two-dimensional shapes can be **open** or **closed**.

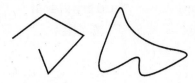

A **polygon** is a closed two-dimensional shape made from line segments that don't cross each other.

polygons

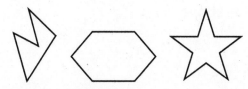

not polygons

A polygon is **concave** if you can connect two points inside the polygon with a line segment that passes outside the polygon. A **convex** polygon has no such line segment. All the inside angles of a convex polygon are less than 180°.

concave   convex

Tell whether each figure is a polygon. If it is not a polygon, explain why it does not fit the definition.

1.

_____

2.

_____

3.

_____

4.

_____

5.

_____

6.

_____

VOCABULARY
regular polygon

▶ Names of Polygons

Polygons are named by the number of sides they have.
Here are some polygons with their names.

triangle	**quadrilateral**	**pentagon**	**hexagon**	**octagon**
3 sides	4 sides	5 sides	6 sides	8 sides

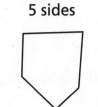 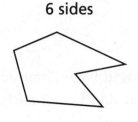 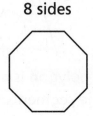

Polygons in which all sides are congruent *and* all angles are
congruent are called **regular polygons**. The octagon above
is a regular octagon.

Name the polygon. Then circle the terms that describe it.

7. _____

regular	not regular
concave	convex

8. _____

regular	not regular
concave	convex

9. 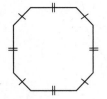 _____

regular	not regular
concave	convex

10. 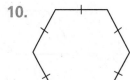 _____

regular	not regular
concave	convex

Write *true* or *false*.

11. A square is a regular quadrilateral. _____

12. It is possible to draw a concave triangle. _____

Attributes of Two-Dimensional Shapes

► Two-Dimensional Shape Cards

2-D shape	2-D shape	2-D shape	2-D shape
A	B	C	D
2-D shape	2-D shape	2-D shape	2-D shape
E	F	G	H
2-D shape	2-D shape	2-D shape	2-D shape
I	J	K	L
2-D shape	2-D shape	2-D shape	2-D shape
M	N	O	P

Attributes of Two-Dimensional Shapes

▶ **Attribute Cards**

concave polygon	convex polygon	straight sides	curved
open	closed	polygon	regular polygon
at least one pair of parallel sides	at least one pair of perpendicular sides	line of symmetry	at least two congruent sides
acute angle	right angle	obtuse angle	angle greater than 180°

Attributes of Two-Dimensional Shapes

Name _____   **Date** _____

▶ Math and Aquariums

A goldfish bowl is a small aquarium. Other aquariums, like those found in museums, can be enormous and have computer monitored and controlled life-support systems.

Many home aquariums are made of glass or acrylic, and are shaped like rectangular prisms. A sketch of Naomi's home aquarium is shown the right.

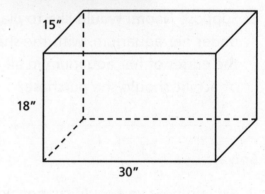

Use the sketch to solve Problems 1 and 2.

1. Which faces of Naomi's aquarium—the top and bottom, the sides, or the front and back—have the greatest perimeter?

   _____

2. Use a formula and find the area of each of the following faces.

   top and bottom _____

   left side and right side _____

   front and back _____

3. Use a formula and find the volume of the aquarium.

   _____

▶ Math and Aquariums (continued)

Residents of salt water aquariums often include colorful fish. Some salt water aquariums also include living plants, rocks, and corals.

Use the sketch of Naomi's aquarium shown below to solve Problems 4–6.

4. Suppose three inches of sand were placed in the bottom of the aquarium. Calculate the remaining volume of the aquarium.

_____

5. Naomi would like to attach rubber edging along the top edges, and along the bottom edges, of her aquarium. Use a formula to determine the minimum length of edging Naomi would need.

_____

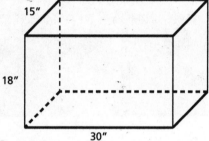

6. Suppose Naomi would like to place a flat sheet of acrylic under her aquarium, with the sheet extending 1-inch beyond the edges of her aquarium in all directions. What size sheet of acrylic should she purchase?

_____

Solve.

7. Explain how you could change your answers to Problem 2 to square feet, and your answer to Problem 3 to cubic feet.

_____

_____

_____

_____

© Houghton Mifflin Harcourt Publishing Company • Image Credits: ©Dinodia Photos/India Images/Alamy Images

▶ Vocabulary

Choose the best term from the box.

1. _____ is the amount of space a solid object occupies. **(Lesson 8-9)**

▶ Concepts and Skills

2. Explain why you multiply to change from centimeters to millimeters. **(Lesson 8-1)**

_____

_____

3. Explain why you divide to change from feet to yards. **(Lesson 8-4)**

_____

_____

Complete. (Lessons 8-1 through 8-6)

4. 0.45 km = _____ m

5. 12.4 mm = _____ cm

6. 63 mL = _____ L

7. _____ L = 14,000 mL

8. _____ mg = 0.032 g

9. _____ in. = $8\frac{1}{2}$ ft

10. 504 in. = _____ yd

11. _____ qt = 13 gal

12. $15\frac{3}{8}$ lb = _____ oz

Use a formula and calculate the volume of each figure.
(Lessons 8-9 through 8-11, 8-13)

13.

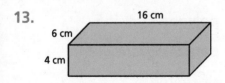

16 cm
6 cm
4 cm

_____

_____

14.

3 mm
12 mm
18 mm

_____

_____

15.

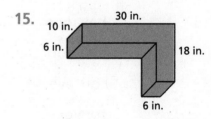

30 in.
10 in.
6 in.
18 in.
6 in.

_____

_____

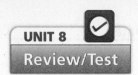

Name _____ Date _____

16. Circle all the names that describe the polygon.

a. (Lesson 8-14)

quadrilateral

rectangle

square

parallelogram

rhombus

trapezoid

b. (Lesson 8-15)

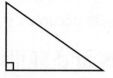

right triangle

obtuse triangle

acute triangle

scalene triangle

isosceles triangle

equilateral triangle

c. (Lesson 8-16)

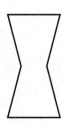

hexagon

octagon

concave

convex

closed

open

d. (Lessons 8-14, 8-16)

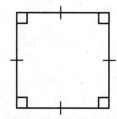

polygon

parallelogram

rectangle

regular

closed

concave

▶ Problem Solving

Solve. (Lessons 8-1 through 8-6)

17. Dr. Florenz needs 25 grams of salt for each student to do an experiment. She has 1.2 kilograms of salt on hand. She has a total of 128 students. How much more salt does she need?

_____

18. Larry ran 220 meters farther than Leigh ran. Leigh ran 2.3 kilometers. How many kilometers did Larry run?

_____

19. Tomas ran 2 miles at track practice. Satomi ran 50 yards more than half as far as Tomas. How many yards did Satomi run?

_____

Use a formula to solve each problem.

20. A paperback book is shaped like a rectangular prism. The cover of the book measures 5 inches by 8 inches, and the book is 2 inches thick. Calculate the volume of the book. (Lessons 8-11, 8-12, 8-17)

_____

21. The cargo space of a railroad boxcar measures 42 feet long by 9 feet wide by 11 feet tall. Find the volume of freight that can be placed in the boxcar. (Lessons 8-11, 8-12, 8-17)

_____

22. A painted line on the highway has a width of $\frac{1}{3}$ foot and covers an area of 900 sq ft. Find the unknown length. (Lessons 8-8, 8-12)

_____

23. Each day at school, Kai records his homework assignments in a small notebook. Each page of the notebook measures $2\frac{1}{4}$ inches by $3\frac{1}{2}$ inches. Find the area of one page. (Lessons 8-8, 8-12, 8-17)

_____

24. Draw a concave pentagon with exactly one pair of perpendicular sides. (Lesson 8-16)

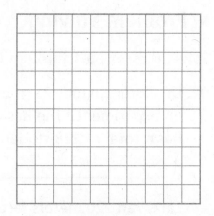

25. **Extended Response** Joel divided the contents of a large bag of granola into smaller bags. He weighed each bag to the nearest $\frac{1}{8}$ pound and recorded the weights in the table on the right. (Lesson 8-7)

Weights of Small Bags of Granola (lb)	
$1\frac{1}{4}$ lb	⫽⫽
$1\frac{3}{8}$ lb	‖
$1\frac{1}{2}$ lb	‖‖
$1\frac{5}{8}$ lb	‖‖
$1\frac{3}{4}$ lb	‖

a. Graph Joel's results on the line plot.

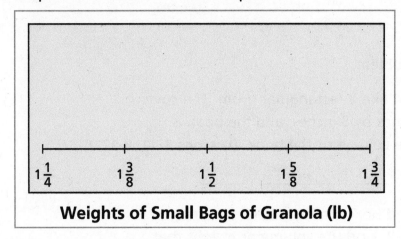

Weights of Small Bags of Granola (lb)

b. How many small bags of granola did Joel make?

_____

c. How many bags weighed less than $1\frac{1}{2}$ lb?

_____

d. If Joel used all of the granola that was in the large bag to make the small bags, how heavy was the large bag of granola when he started? Explain your thinking.

_____

_____

Reference Tables

Table of Measures

Metric	Customary

Length/Area/Volume

Metric	Customary
1 millimeter (mm) = 0.001 meter (m)	1 foot (ft) = 12 inches (in.)
1 centimeter (cm) = 0.01 meter	1 yard (yd) = 36 inches
1 decimeter (dm) = 0.1 meter	1 yard = 3 feet
1 dekameter (dam) = 10 meters	1 mile (mi) = 5,280 feet
1 hectometer (hm) = 100 meters	1 mile = 1,760 yards
1 kilometer (km) = 1,000 meters	1 acre = 4,840 square yards
1 hectare (ha) = 1,000 square meters (m^2)	1 acre = 43,560 square feet
1 square centimeter = 1 sq cm A metric unit for measuring area. It is the area of a square that is 1 centimeter on each side.	1 acre = $\frac{1}{640}$ square mile
	1 square inch = 1 sq in. A customary unit for measuring area. It is the area of a square that is 1 inch on each side.
1 cubic centimeter = 1 cu cm A unit for measuring volume. It is the volume of a cube with each edge 1 centimeter long.	1 cubic inch = 1 cu in. A unit for measuring volume. It is the volume of a cube with each edge 1 inch long.

Capacity

Metric	Customary
1 milliliter (mL) = 0.001 liter (L)	1 teaspoon (tsp) = $\frac{1}{6}$ fluid ounce (fl oz)
1 centiliter (cL) = 0.01 liter	1 tablespoon (tbsp) = $\frac{1}{2}$ fluid ounce
1 deciliter (dL) = 0.1 liter	1 cup (c) = 8 fluid ounces
1 dekaliter (daL) = 10 liters	1 pint (pt) = 2 cups
1 hectoliter (hL) = 100 liters	1 quart (qt) = 2 pints
1 kiloliter (kL) = 1,000 liters	1 gallon (gal) = 4 quarts

Mass / Weight

Mass	Weight
1 milligram (mg) = 0.001 gram (g)	1 pound (lb) = 16 ounces
1 centigram (cg) = 0.01 gram	1 ton (T) = 2,000 pounds
1 decigram (dg) = 0.1 gram	
1 dekagram (dag) = 10 grams	
1 hectogram (hg) = 100 grams	
1 kilogram (kg) = 1,000 grams	
1 metric ton = 1,000 kilograms	

Volume/Capacity/Mass for Water

1 cubic centimeter = 1 milliliter = 1 gram

1,000 cubic centimeters = 1 liter = 1 kilogram

Reference Tables (continued)

Table of Units of Time

Time

1 minute (min) = 60 seconds (sec)

1 hour (hr) = 60 minutes

1 day = 24 hours

1 week (wk) = 7 days

1 month is about 30 days

1 year (yr) = 12 months (mo)
 or about 52 weeks

1 year = 365 days

1 leap year = 366 days

1 decade = 10 years

1 century = 100 years

1 millennium = 1,000 years

Table of Formulas

Perimeter

Polygon $P = $ sum of the lengths of the sides

Rectangle $P = 2(l + w)$ or $P = 2l + 2w$

Square $P = 4s$

Area

Rectangle $A = l \cdot w$

Square $A = s \cdot s$ or $A = s^2$

Volume of a Rectangular Prism

$$V = lwh \text{ or } V = Bh$$
(where B is the area of the base of the prism)

Properties of Operations

Associative Property of Addition
$$(a + b) + c = a + (b + c) \qquad (2 + 5) + 3 = 2 + (5 + 3)$$

Commutative Property of Addition
$$a + b = b + a \qquad 4 + 6 = 6 + 4$$

Additive Identity Property of 0
$$a + 0 = 0 + a = a \qquad 3 + 0 = 0 + 3 = 3$$

Associative Property of Multiplication
$$(a \cdot b) \cdot c = a \cdot (b \cdot c) \qquad (3 \cdot 5) \cdot 7 = 3 \cdot (5 \cdot 7)$$

Commutative Property of Multiplication
$$a \cdot b = b \cdot a \qquad 6 \cdot 3 = 3 \cdot 6$$

Multiplicative Identity Property of 1
$$a \cdot 1 = 1 \cdot a = a \qquad 8 \cdot 1 = 1 \cdot 8 = 8$$

Multiplicative Inverse
For every $a \neq 0$ there exists $\frac{1}{a}$ so that $a \cdot \frac{1}{a} = \frac{1}{a} \cdot a = 1$.

For $a = 5$, $5 \cdot \frac{1}{5} = \frac{1}{5} \cdot 5 = 1$.

Distributive Property of Multiplication over Addition
$$a \cdot (b + c) = (a \cdot b) + (a \cdot c) \qquad 2 \cdot (4 + 3) = (2 \cdot 4) + (2 \cdot 3)$$

Order of Operations

Step 1 Perform operations inside parentheses.

Step 2 Simplify powers.*

Step 3 Multiply and divide from left to right.

Step 4 Add and subtract from left to right.

*Grade 5 does not include simplifying expressions with exponents.

Problem Types

Addition and Subtraction Problem Types

	Result Unknown	Change Unknown	Start Unknown
Add to	A glass contained $\frac{2}{3}$ cup of orange juice. Then $\frac{1}{4}$ cup of pineapple juice was added. How much juice is in the glass now? *Situation and solution equation:*[1] $\frac{2}{3} + \frac{1}{4} = c$	A glass contained $\frac{2}{3}$ cup of orange juice. Then some pineapple juice was added. Now the glass contains $\frac{11}{12}$ cup of juice. How much pineapple juice was added? *Situation equation:* $\frac{2}{3} + c = \frac{11}{12}$ *Solution equation:* $c = \frac{11}{12} - \frac{2}{3}$	A glass contained some orange juice. Then $\frac{1}{4}$ cup of pineapple juice was added. Now the glass contains $\frac{11}{12}$ cup of juice. How much orange juice was in the glass to start? *Situation equation* $c + \frac{1}{4} = \frac{11}{12}$ *Solution equation:* $c = \frac{11}{12} - \frac{1}{4}$
Take from	Micah had a ribbon $\frac{5}{6}$ yard long. He cut off a piece $\frac{1}{3}$ yard long. What is the length of the ribbon that is left? *Situation and solution equation:* $\frac{5}{6} - \frac{1}{3} = r$	Micah had a ribbon $\frac{5}{6}$ yard long. He cut off a piece. Now the ribbon is $\frac{1}{2}$ yard long. What is the length of the ribbon he cut off? *Situation equation:* $\frac{5}{6} - r = \frac{1}{2}$ *Solution equation:* $r = \frac{5}{6} - \frac{1}{2}$	Micah had a ribbon. He cut off a piece $\frac{1}{3}$ yard long. Now the ribbon is $\frac{1}{2}$ yard long. What was the length of the ribbon he started with? *Situation equation:* $r - \frac{1}{3} = \frac{1}{2}$ *Solution equation:* $r = \frac{1}{2} + \frac{1}{3}$

[1]A situation equation represents the structure (action) in the problem situation. A solution equation shows the operation used to find the answer.

	Total Unknown	Addend Unknown	Both Addends Unknown
Put Together/ Take Apart	A baker combines $\frac{3}{4}$ cup of white flour and $\frac{1}{2}$ cup of wheat flour. How much flour is this altogether? *Math drawing:*[2] f $\frac{3}{4}$ $\frac{1}{2}$ *Situation and solution equation:* $\frac{3}{4} + \frac{1}{2} = f$	Of the $1\frac{1}{4}$ cups of flour a baker uses, $\frac{3}{4}$ cup is white flour. The rest is wheat flour. How much wheat flour does the baker use? *Math drawing:* $1\frac{1}{4}$ $\frac{3}{4}$ f *Situation equation:* $1\frac{1}{4} = \frac{3}{4} + f$ *Solution equation:* $f = 1\frac{1}{4} - \frac{3}{4}$	A baker uses $1\frac{1}{4}$ cups of flour. Some is white flour and some is wheat flour. How much of each type of flour does the baker use? *Math drawing:* $1\frac{1}{4}$ f w *Situation equation* $1\frac{1}{4} = f + w$

[2]These math drawings are called math mountains in Grades 1–3 and break-apart drawings in Grades 4 and 5.

Problem Types continued

Addition and Subtraction Problem Types

	Difference Unknown	Greater Unknown	Smaller Unknown
Additive Comparison[1]	**Using "More"** At a zoo, the female rhino weighs $1\frac{3}{4}$ tons. The male rhino weighs $2\frac{1}{2}$ tons. How much more does the male rhino weigh than the female rhino? **Using "Less"** At a zoo, the female rhino weighs $1\frac{3}{4}$ tons. The male rhino weighs $2\frac{1}{2}$ tons. How much less does the female rhino weigh than the male rhino?	**Leading Language** At a zoo, the female rhino weighs $1\frac{3}{4}$ tons. The male rhino weighs $\frac{3}{4}$ tons more than the female rhino. How much does the male rhino weigh? **Misleading Language** At a zoo, the female rhino weighs $1\frac{3}{4}$ tons. The female rhino weighs $\frac{3}{4}$ tons less than the male rhino. How much does the male rhino weigh?	**Leading Language** At a zoo, the male rhino weighs $2\frac{1}{2}$ tons. The female rhino weighs $\frac{3}{4}$ tons less than the male rhino. How much does the female rhino weigh? **Misleading Language** At a zoo, the male rhino weighs $2\frac{1}{2}$ tons. The male rhino weighs $\frac{3}{4}$ tons more than the female rhino. How much does the female rhino weigh?

Math drawing:

$2\frac{1}{2}$		
$1\frac{3}{4}$	d	

Situation equation:
$1\frac{3}{4} + d = 2\frac{1}{2}$ or
$d = 2\frac{1}{2} - 1\frac{3}{4}$
Solution equation:
$d = 2\frac{1}{2} - 1\frac{3}{4}$

Math drawing:

m	
$1\frac{3}{4}$	$\frac{3}{4}$

Situation and solution equation:
$1\frac{3}{4} + \frac{3}{4} = m$

Math drawing:

$2\frac{1}{2}$	
f	$\frac{3}{4}$

Situation equation
$f + \frac{3}{4} = 2\frac{1}{2}$ or
$f = 2\frac{1}{2} - \frac{3}{4}$
Solution equation:
$f = 2\frac{1}{2} - \frac{3}{4}$

[1]A comparison sentence can always be said in two ways. One way uses *more*, and the other uses *fewer* or *less*. Misleading language suggests the wrong operation. For example, it says the *female rhino weighs* $\frac{3}{4}$ *tons less than the male*, but you have to add $\frac{3}{4}$ tons to the female's weight to get the male's weight

Multiplication and Division Problem Types[1]

	Unknown Product	Group Size Unknown	Number of Groups Unknown
Equal Groups	Maddie ran around a $\frac{1}{4}$-mile track 16 times. How far did she run? *Situation and solution equation:* $n = 16 \cdot \frac{1}{4}$	Maddie ran around a track 16 times. She ran 4 miles in all. What is the distance around the track? *Situation equation:* $16 \cdot n = 4$ *Solution equation:* $n = 4 \div 16$	Maddie ran around a $\frac{1}{4}$-mile track. She ran a total distance of 4 miles. How many times did she run around the track? *Situation equation* $n \cdot \frac{1}{4} = 4$ *Solution equation:* $n = 4 \div \frac{1}{4}$

	Unknown Product	Unknown Factor	Unknown Factor
Arrays[2]	An auditorium has 58 rows with 32 seats in each row. How many seats are in the auditorium? *Math drawing:* 32 / 58 / s *Situation and solution equation:* $s = 58 \cdot 32$	An auditorium has 58 rows with the same number of seats in each row. There are 1,856 seats in all. How many seats are in each row? *Math drawing:* s / 58 / 1,856 *Situation equation:* $58 \cdot s = 1,856$ *Solution equation:* $s = 1,856 \div 58$	The 1,856 seats in an auditorium are arranged in rows of 32. How many rows of seats are there? *Math drawing:* 32 / s / 1,856 *Situation equation* $s \cdot 32 = 1,856$ *Solution equation:* $s = 1,856 \div 32$

[1]In Grade 5, students solve three types of fraction division problems: 1) They divide two whole numbers in cases where the quotient is a fraction; 2) They divide a whole number by a unit fraction; 3) They divide a unit fraction by a whole number. Fraction division with non-unit fractions is introduced in Grade 6.

[2]We use rectangle models for both array and area problems in Grades 5 and 6 because the numbers in the problems are too large to represent with arrays.

Multiplication and Division Problem Types

	Unknown Product	Unknown Factor	Unknown Factor
Area	A poster has a length of 1.2 meters and a width of 0.7 meter. What is the area of the poster? *Math drawing:* 1.2 0.7 | A *Situation and solution equation:* $A = 1.2 \cdot 0.7$	A poster has an area of 0.84 square meters. The length of the poster is 1.2 meters. What is the width of the poster? *Math drawing:* 1.2 w | 0.84 *Situation equation:* $1.2 \cdot w = 0.84$ *Solution equation:* $w = 0.84 \div 1.2$	A poster has an area of 0.84 square meters. The width of the poster is 0.7 meter. What is the length of the poster? *Math drawing:* l 0.7 | 0.84 *Situation equation* $l \cdot 0.7 = 0.84$ *Solution equation:* $l = 0.84 \div 0.7$

	Unknown Product	Unknown Factor	Unknown Factor
Multiplicative Comparison	**Whole Number Multiplier** Sam has 5 times as many goldfish as Brady has. Brady has 3 goldfish. How many goldfish does Sam have? *Math drawing:* s | 3 | 3 | 3 | 3 | 3 | b | 3 | *Situation and solution equation:* $s = 5 \cdot 3$	**Whole Number Multiplier** Sam has 5 times as many goldfish as Brady has. Sam has 15 goldfish. How many goldfish does Brady have? *Math drawing:* 15 s |---|---|---|---| b |___| *Situation equation:* $5 \cdot b = 15$ *Solution equation:* $b = 15 \div 5$	**Whole Number Multiplier** Sam has 15 goldfish. Brady has 3 goldfish. The number of goldfish Sam has is how many times the number Brady has? *Math drawing:* 15 s | 3 | 3 | 3 | 3 | 3 | b | 3 | *Situation equation* $n \cdot 3 = 15$ *Solution equation:* $n = 15 \div 3$
	Fractional Multiplier Brady has $\frac{1}{5}$ times as many goldfish as Sam has. Sam has 15 goldfish. How many goldfish does Brady have? *Math drawing:* 15 s |---|---|---|---| b |___| $\frac{1}{5}$ of 15 *Situation and solution equation:* $b = \frac{1}{5} \cdot 15$	**Fractional Multiplier** Brady has $\frac{1}{5}$ times as many goldfish as Sam has. Brady has 3 goldfish. How many goldfish does Sam have? *Math drawing:* s |---|---|---|---| b | 3 | $\frac{1}{5}$ of s *Situation equation:* $\frac{1}{5} \cdot s = 3$ *Solution equation:* $s = 3 \div \frac{1}{5}$	**Fractional Multiplier** Sam has 15 goldfish. Brady has 3 goldfish. The number of goldfish Brady has is how many times the number Sam has? *Math drawing:* 15 s | 3 | 3 | 3 | 3 | 3 | b | 3 | *Situation equation:* $n \cdot 15 = 3$ *Solution equation:* $n = 3 \div 15$

Vocabulary Activities

▶ Word Review [PAIRS]

Work with a partner. Choose a word from a current unit or a review word from a previous unit. Use the word to complete one of the activities listed on the right. Then ask your partner if they have any edits to your work or questions about what you described. Repeat, having your partner choose a word.

Activities

▶ Give the meaning in words or gestures.

▶ Use the word in the sentence.

▶ Give another word that is related to the word in some way and explain the relationship.

▶ Crossword Puzzle [PAIRS] OR [INDIVIDUALS]

Create a crossword puzzle similar to the example below. Use vocabulary words from the unit. You can add other related words, too. Challenge your partner to solve the puzzle.

Crossword grid:

Across: ¹d-i-v-i-[a]-e-n (down from d), ²s-u-m across; ²s-u-b-t-r-a-c-t-i-o-n (down); ⁴a-d-d-i-t-i-o-n across; ³u-n-i-t (down); ⁵a-d-d across; ⁶g-r-o-u-p across with n below.

Across

2. The answer to an addition problem

4. _____ and subtraction are inverse operations.

5. To put amounts together

6. When you trade 10 ones for 1 ten, you _____.

Down

1. The number to be divided in a division problem

2. The operation that you can use to find out how much more one number is than another.

3. A fraction with a numerator of 1 is a _____ fraction.

▶ Word Wall   PAIRS   OR   SMALL GROUPS

With your teacher's permission, start a word wall in your classroom. As you work through each lesson, put the math vocabulary words on index cards and place them on the word wall. You can work with a partner or a small group to choose a word and give the definition.

▶ Word Web   INDIVIDUALS

Make a word web for a word or words you do not understand in a unit. Fill in the web with words or phrases that are related to the vocabulary word.

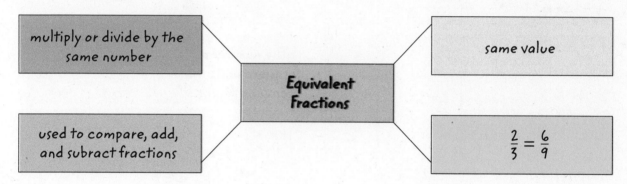

▶ Alphabet Challenge   PAIRS   OR   INDIVIDUALS

Take an alphabet challenge. Choose three letters from the alphabet. Think of three vocabulary words for each letter. Then write the definition or draw an example for each word.

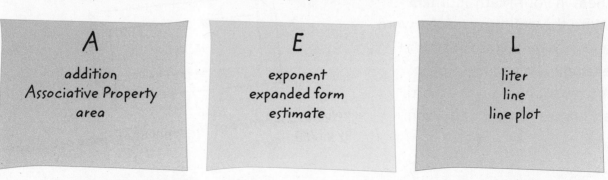

Vocabulary Activities (continued)

▶ Concentration [PAIRS]

Write the vocabulary words and related words from a unit on index cards. Write the definitions on a different set of index cards. Mix up both sets of cards. Then place the cards facedown on a table in an array, for example, 3 by 3 or 3 by 4. Take turns turning over two cards. If one card is a word and one card is a definition that matches the word, take the pair. Continue until each word has been matched with its definition.

area

The number of square units that cover a figure.

▶ Math Journal [INDIVIDUALS]

As you learn new words, write them in your Math Journal. Write the definition of the word and include a sketch or an example. As you learn new information about the word, add notes to your definition.

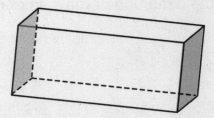

rectangular prism: a solid figure with two rectangular bases that are congruent and parallel

volume: a measure of the amount of space occupied by a solid figure

► What's the Word? [PAIRS]

Work together to make a poster or bulletin board display of
the words in a unit. Write definitions on a set of index cards.
Mix up the cards. Work with a partner, choosing a definition
from the index cards. Have your partner point to the word
on the poster and name the matching math vocabulary word.
Switch roles and try the activity again.

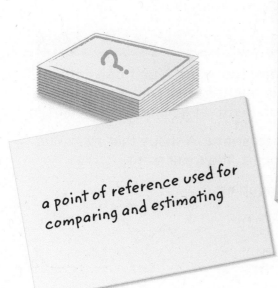

estimate

round

mixed number

equivalent fraction

common denominator

benchmark

simplify a fraction

unsimplify a fraction

unit fraction

a point of reference used for comparing and estimating

Glossary

acute triangle A triangle with three acute angles.

Examples:

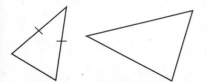

additive comparison A comparison in which one quantity is an amount greater or less than another. An additive comparison can be represented by an addition equation.

Example: Josh has 5 more goldfish than Tia.

$$j = t + 5$$

area The number of square units that cover a two-dimensional figure without gaps or overlap.

Example:

Area = 3 cm × 5 cm = 15 sq. cm

5 cm

3 cm

Associative Property of Addition Changing the grouping of addends does not change the sum. In symbols, $(a + b) + c = a + (b + c)$ for any numbers a, b, and c.

Example:

$(4.7 + 2.6) + 1.4 = 4.7 + (2.6 + 1.4)$

Associative Property of Multiplication Changing the grouping of factors does not change the product. In symbols, $(a \cdot b) \cdot c = a \cdot (b \cdot c)$ for any numbers a, b, and c.

Example:

$(0.73 \cdot 0.2) \cdot 5 = 0.73 \cdot (0.2 \cdot 5)$

B

base In a power, the number that is used as a repeated factor.

Example: In the power 10^3, the base is 10.

benchmark A point of reference used for comparing and estimating. The numbers 0, $\frac{1}{2}$, and 1 are common fraction benchmarks.

C

centimeter (cm) A unit of length in the metric system that equals one hundredth of a meter. 1 cm = 0.01 m.

closed shape A shape that starts and ends at the same point.

Examples:

common denominator A common multiple of two or more denominators.

Example: 18 is a common denominator of $\frac{2}{3}$ and $\frac{5}{6}$.

$$\frac{2}{3} = \frac{12}{18} \text{ and } \frac{5}{6} = \frac{15}{18}$$

Commutative Property of Addition
Changing the order of addends does not change the sum. In symbols, $a + b = b + a$ for any numbers a and b.

Example: $\frac{3}{5} + \frac{4}{9} = \frac{4}{9} + \frac{3}{5}$

Commutative Property of Multiplication Changing the order of factors does not change the product. In symbols, $a \cdot b = b \cdot a$ for any numbers a and b.

Example: $\frac{3}{7} \cdot \frac{4}{5} = \frac{4}{5} \cdot \frac{3}{7}$

comparison A statement, model, or drawing that shows the relationship between two quantities.

comparison bars Bars that represent the greater amount and the lesser amount in a comparison situation.

Example: Sarah made 2 quarts of soup. Ryan made 6 quarts. These comparison bars show that Ryan made 3 times as many quarts as Sarah.

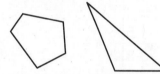

Ryan (r) | 2 | 2 | 2 | 6

Sarah (s) | 2

composite solid A solid figure made by combining two or more basic solid figures.

Example: The composite solid on the left below is composed of two rectangular prisms, as shown on the right.

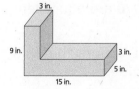
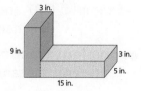

concave polygon A polygon for which you can connect two points inside the polygon with a segment that passes outside the polygon. A concave polygon has a "dent."

Examples:

convex polygon A polygon that is not concave. All the inside angles of a convex polygon have a measure less than 180°.

Examples:

coordinate plane A system of coordinates formed by the perpendicular intersection of horizontal and vertical number lines.

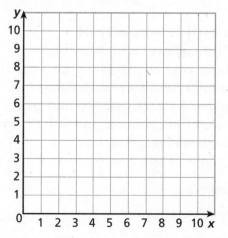

Glossary (continued)

cubic unit The volume of a unit cube. A cubic unit is a unit for measuring volume.

D

decimal A number that includes a decimal point separating the whole number part of the number from the fraction part of the number.

Examples:

7.3	seven and three tenths
42.081	forty-two and eighty-one thousandths

decimeter (dm) A unit of length in the metric system that equals one tenth of a meter. 1 dm = 0.1 m.

Digit-by-Digit Method A method for solving division problems.

Example:

```
       546
   7 ) 3,822
     − 3,5
     ──────
        32
      − 28
      ──────
        42
      − 42
      ──────
```

Distributive Property of Multiplication Over Addition Multiplying a number by a sum gives the same result as multiplying the number by each addend and then adding the products. In symbols, for all numbers a, b, and c:
$$a \times (b + c) = a \times b + a \times c$$

Example:
$$4 \times (2 + 0.75) = 4 \times 2 + 4 \times 0.75$$

dividend The number that is divided in a division problem.

Example:

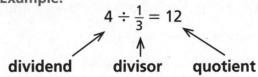
$$4 \div \tfrac{1}{3} = 12$$
dividend   divisor   quotient

divisor The number you divide by in a division problem.

Example:

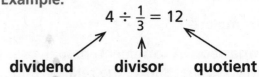
$$4 \div \tfrac{1}{3} = 12$$
dividend   divisor   quotient

E

edge A line segment where two faces of a three-dimensional figure meet.

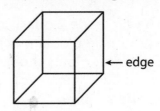
← edge

equilateral triangle A triangle with three sides of the same length.

Example:

equivalent decimals Decimals that represent the same value.

Example: 0.07 and 0.070 are equivalent decimals.

equivalent fractions Fractions that represent the same value.

Example: $\frac{1}{2}$ and $\frac{3}{6}$ are equivalent fractions.

estimate Find *about* how many or *about* how much, often by using rounding or benchmarks.

evaluate To substitute values for the variables in an expression and then simplify the resulting expression.

Example:

Evaluate $7 + 5 \cdot n$ for $n = 2$.

$7 + 5 \cdot n = 7 + 5 \cdot 2$ Substitute 2 for n.

$\quad\quad\quad = 7 + 10$ Multiply.

$\quad\quad\quad = 17$ Add

expanded form A way of writing a number that shows the value of each of its digits.

Example: The expanded form of 35.026 is $30 + 5 + 0.02 + 0.006$.

expanded form (powers of 10) A way of writing a number that shows the value of each of its digits using powers of 10.

Example: The expanded form of 35.026 using powers of 10 is

$(3 \times 10) + (5 \times 1) + (2 \times 0.01) + (6 + 0.001)$

Expanded Notation Method A method for solving multidigit multiplication and division problems.

Examples:

```
    43
  × 67
 2,400
   280
   180
    21
 2,881
```

```
      6 )
     40   546
    500
  7) 3,822
   -3,500
      322
     -280
       42
      -42
```

exponent In a power, the number that tells how many times the base is used as a factor.

Example: In the power 10^3, the exponent is 3.
$10^3 = 10 \times 10 \times 10$

exponential form The representation of a number that uses a base and an exponent.

Example: The exponential form of 100 is 10^2.

expression A combination of one or more numbers, variables, or numbers and variables, with one or more operations.

Examples: 4

t

$6 \cdot n$

$4 \div p + 5$

$5 \times 4 + 3 \times 7$

$6 \cdot (x + 2)$

F

face A flat surface of a three-dimensional figure.

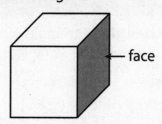

← face

factor One of two or more numbers multiplied to get a product.

Example:

$$\frac{3}{5} \cdot 10 = 6$$

factor   factor   product

© Houghton Mifflin Harcourt Publishing Company

Glossary (continued)

frequency table A table that shows how many times each outcome, item, or category occurs.

Example:

Outcome	Number of Students
1	6
2	3
3	5
4	4
5	2
6	5

G

greater than (>) A symbol used to show how two numbers compare. The greater number goes before the > symbol and the lesser number goes after.

Example: $\frac{2}{3} > \frac{1}{2}$ Two thirds is greater than one half.

H

hundredth A unit fraction representing one of one hundred equal parts of a whole, written as 0.01 or $\frac{1}{100}$.

I

isosceles triangle A triangle with at least two sides of the same length.

Examples:

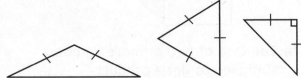

L

less than (<) A symbol used to show how two numbers compare. The lesser number goes before the < symbol and the greater number goes after.

Example: $\frac{1}{4} < \frac{1}{3}$ One fourth is less than one third.

line plot A diagram that uses a number line to show the frequency of data.

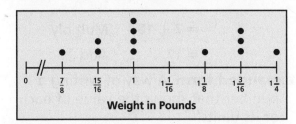

Weight in Pounds

M

meter The basic unit of length in the metric system.

mile (mi) A customary unit of length equal to 5,280 feet or 1,760 yards.

millimeter (mm) A unit of length in the metric system that equals one thousandth of a meter.
1 mm = 0.001 m.

mixed number A number with a whole number part and a fraction part.

Example: The mixed number $3\frac{2}{5}$ means $3 + \frac{2}{5}$.

multiplier The number the numerator and denominator of a fraction are multiplied by to get an equivalent fraction.

Example: A multiplier of 5 changes $\frac{2}{3}$ to $\frac{10}{15}$.

multiplicative comparison
A comparison in which one quantity is a number of times the size of another. A multiplicative comparison can be represented by a multiplication equation or a division equation.

Example: Tomás picked 3 times as many apples as Catie.

$$t = 3 \cdot c$$

$$t \div 3 = c \text{ or } \frac{1}{3} \cdot t = c$$

N

New Groups Below Method A method used to solve multidigit multiplication problems.

Example:

$$
\begin{array}{r}
67 \\
\times\ 43 \\
\hline
12 \\
81 \\
2\ 2 \\
480 \\
1 \\
\hline
2{,}881
\end{array}
$$

numerical pattern A sequence of numbers that share a relationship.

Example: In this numerical pattern, each term is 3 more than the term before.

2, 5, 8, 11, 14, . . .

O

obtuse triangle A triangle with an obtuse angle.

Examples:

one-dimensional figure A figure with only one dimension, usually length.

Examples:

open shape A shape that does not start and end at the same point.

Examples:

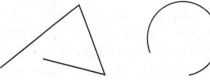

Order of Operations A rule that states the order in which the operations in an expression should be done:

Step 1 Perform operations inside parentheses.

Step 2 Multiply and divide from left to right.

Step 3 Add and subtract from left to right.

ordered pair A pair of numbers that shows the position of a point on a coordinate plane.

Example: The ordered pair (3, 4) represents a point 3 units to the right of the y-axis and 4 units above the x-axis.

origin The point (0, 0) on the coordinate plane.

overestimate An estimate that is too big.

Glossary (continued)

P

parallelogram A quadrilateral with two pairs of parallel sides.

Examples:

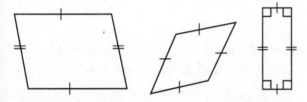

partial products In a multidigit multiplication problem, the products obtained by multiplying each place value of one factor by each place value of the other.

Example: In the problem below, the partial products are in red.

$$25 \cdot 53 = 20 \cdot 50 + 20 \cdot 3 + 5 \cdot 50 + 5 \cdot 3$$

perimeter The distance around a figure.

Example:

Perimeter $= 2 \cdot 3$ cm $+ 2 \cdot 5$ cm $= 16$ cm

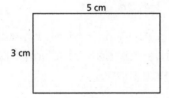

Place Value Rows Method A method used to solve multidigit multiplication problems.

Example:

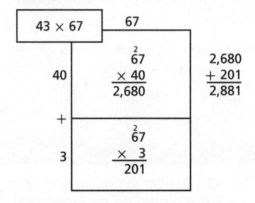

Place Value Sections Method A method used to solve multidigit multiplication and division problems.

Examples:

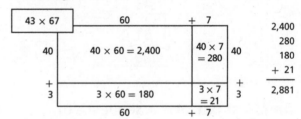

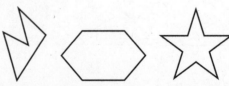

polygon A closed two-dimensional shape made from line segments that do not cross each other.

Examples:

power of 10 A power with a base of 10. A number in the form 10^n.

Examples: 10^1, 10^2, 10^3

product The result of a multiplication.

Example:

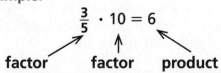

rectangular prism A solid figure with two rectangular bases that are congruent and parallel.

Example:

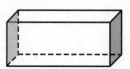

Q

quadrilateral A closed two-dimensional shape with four straight sides.

Examples:

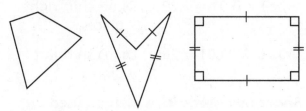

quotient The answer to a division problem.

Example:

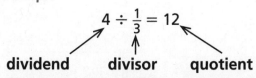

R

rectangle A parallelogram with four right angles.

Examples:

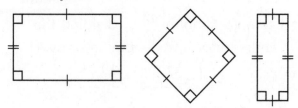

regular polygon A polygon in which all sides and all angles are congruent.

Examples:

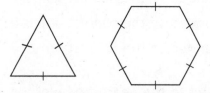

remainder The number left over when a divisor does not divide evenly into a dividend.

Example:

$$
\begin{array}{r}
13 \\
7\overline{)94} \\
-7 \\
\hline
24 \\
21 \\
\hline
3 \leftarrow \text{remainder}
\end{array}
$$

rhombus A parallelogram with four congruent sides.

Examples:

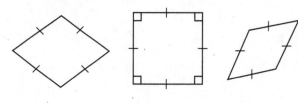

Glossary (continued)

right triangle A triangle with a right angle.

Examples:

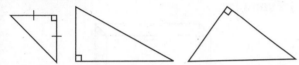

round To change a number to a nearby number.

Examples:

54.72 rounded to the nearest ten is 50.

54.72 rounded to the nearest one is 55.

54.72 rounded to the nearest tenth is 54.7.

$3\frac{7}{9}$ rounded to the nearest whole number is 4.

S

scalene triangle A triangle with no sides of the same length.

Examples:

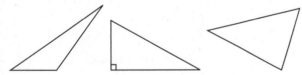

shift To change position. When we multiply a decimal or whole number by 10, 100, or 1,000, the digits shift to the left. When we divide by 10, 100, or 1,000, the digits shift to the right. When we multiply by 0.1, 0.01, or 0.001, the digits shift to the right. When we divide by 0.1, 0.01, or 0.001, the digits shift to the left.

Examples:

$72.4 \times 100 = 7,240$ Digits shift left 2 places.

$5.04 \div 10 = 0.504$ Digits shift right 1 place.

$729 \times 0.01 = 7.29$ Digits shift right 2 places.

$0.26 \div 0.001 = 260$ Digits shift left 3 places.

Short Cut Method A method used to solve multidigit multiplication problems.

Example:

$$\begin{array}{r} \overset{1}{}\overset{2}{} \\ 43 \\ \times\ 67 \\ \hline 301 \\ 2,580 \\ \hline 2,881 \end{array}$$

simplify a fraction Make an equivalent fraction by dividing the numerator and denominator of a fraction by the same number. Simplifying makes fewer but larger parts.

Example: Simplify $\frac{12}{16}$ by dividing the numerator and denominator by 4.

$$\frac{12 \div 4}{16 \div 4} = \frac{3}{4}$$

simplify an expression Use the Order of Operations to find the value of the expression.

Example: Simplify $6 \cdot (2 + 5) \div 3$.

$$6 \cdot (2 + 5) \div 3 = 6 \cdot 7 \div 3$$
$$= 42 \div 3$$
$$= 14$$

situation equation An equation that shows the action or the relationship in a word problem.

Example:

Liam has some change in his pocket. He spends 25¢. Now he has 36¢ in his pocket. How much change did he have to start?

situation equation: $x - 25 = 36$

solution equation An equation that shows the operation to perform in order to solve a word problem.

Example:

Liam has some change in his pocket. He spends 25¢. Now he has 36¢ in his pocket. How much change did he have to start?

solution equation: $x = 36 + 25$

square A rectangle with four congruent sides. (Or, a rhombus with four right angles.)

Examples:

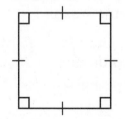 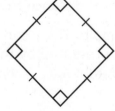

standard form The form of a number using digits, in which the place of each digit indicates its value.

Example: 407.65

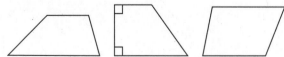

tenth A unit fraction representing one of ten equal parts of a whole, written as 0.1 or $\frac{1}{10}$.

term Each number in a numerical pattern.

Example: In the pattern below, 3 is the first term, and 9 is the fourth term.

3, 5, 7, 9, 11, . . .

thousandth A unit fraction representing one of one thousand equal parts of a whole, written as 0.001 or $\frac{1}{1,000}$.

three-dimensional figure A figure with three dimensions, usually length, width, and height.

Examples:

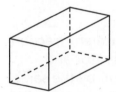

ton (T) A customary unit of weight that equals 2,000 pounds.

trapezoid A quadrilateral with exactly one pair of parallel sides.

Examples:

two-dimensional figure A figure with two dimensions, usually length and width.

Examples:

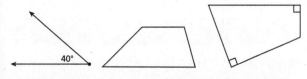

U

underestimate An estimate that is too small.

unit cube A cube with sides lengths of 1 unit.

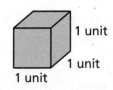

1 unit
1 unit
1 unit

unit fraction A fraction with a numerator of 1. A unit fraction is one equal part of a whole.

Examples: $\frac{1}{3}$ and $\frac{1}{12}$

unsimplify Make an equivalent fraction by multiplying the numerator and denominator of a fraction by the same number. Unsimplifying makes more but smaller parts.

Example: Unsimplify $\frac{3}{4}$ by multiplying the numerator and denominator by 2.

$$\frac{3 \times 2}{4 \times 2} = \frac{6}{8}$$

V

variable A letter or other symbol used to stand for an unknown number in an algebraic expression.

volume A measure of the amount of space occupied by a solid figure. Volume is measured in cubic units.

W

word form The form of a number that uses words instead of digits.

Example: twelve and thirty-two hundredths

X

x-axis The horizontal axis of the coordinate plane.

x-coordinate The first number in an ordered pair, which represents a point's horizontal distance from the y-axis.

Example: The x-coordinate of the point represented by the ordered pair (3, 4) is 3.

Y

y-axis The vertical axis of the coordinate plane.

y-coordinate The second number in an ordered pair, which represents a point's vertical distance from the x-axis.

Example: The y-coordinate of the point represented by the ordered pair (3, 4) is 4.